Rescue Boat

*True Stories of Rescues, Fishing,
and Adventures on the Water*

Hal Records
Robert Behling

Rescue Boat: True Stories of Rescues, Fishing,
and Adventures on the Water
Copyright © 2021 Hal Records and Robert Behling.
Produced and printed
by Stillwater River Publications.

Visit our website at
www.StillwaterPress.com
for more information.
First Stillwater River Publications Edition
Library of Congress Control Number: 2020925906
Paperback ISBN: 978-1-952521-96-6
1 2 3 4 5 6 7 8 9 10
Written by Hal Records and Robert Behling.
Published by Stillwater River Publications,
Pawtucket, RI, USA.
Publisher's Cataloging-In-Publication Data
(Prepared by The Donohue Group, Inc.)

Names: Records, Hal, author. | Behling, Robert, 1938- au-
    thor.
Title: Rescue boat : true stories of rescues, fishing, and ad-
    ventures on the water / Hal Records [and] Robert
    Behling.
Description: First Stillwater River Publications edition. |
    Pawtucket, RI, USA : Stillwater River Publications,
    [2021] | Includes index.
Identifiers: ISBN 9781952521966 (paperback)
Subjects: LCSH: Boating accidents--Anecdotes. | Boats and
    boating--Anecdotes. | Fishing accidents--Anecdotes. |
    Rescues--Anecdotes. | LCGFT: Anecdotes.
Classification: LCC GV777.55 .R47 2021 | DDC
    797.1028/9--dc23

*The views and opinions expressed in this book
are solely those of the author
and do not necessarily reflect the
views and opinions of the publisher.*

Table of Contents

Part 3: Getting Seasoned

Foreword

Captain Hal and Captain Bob grew up on the water, Hal on the Atlantic Ocean and Connecticut ponds, Bob on both the Hudson and Croton Rivers. They grew up loving the water, and this love continues to this day. What makes this partnership work is Hal enjoys boats of all kinds, has an inquisitive and calculating mind, and enjoys a little risk and danger. Bob thinks of a boat as a platform for catching game fish, but is willing to try new things like sailing. He also enjoys telling stories and sharing experiences. The two captains play well off each other, and their synergy strengthens the stories you are about to read. We have chosen to highlight rescue boat work because Captain Hal's stories and experiences bring to life the thrill of being on the water in all kinds of situations, and hence the clever title of the book: *Rescue Boat*. As used in this book, the terms "rescue boat" and "rescue boat service" refer to vessels and crews of the United States Coast Guard, police, fire, environmental agencies, harbormasters, and marine towing and salvage companies. Wherever you are in the United States, these organizations are working to help make your boating experience safer.

Boating is easy to learn. Captain Hal was told by an old salt at an early age that he would teach him how to boat and sail in half an hour...and then Hal would spend the rest of his life getting good at it. Little did he know at the time how right on the old salt was. Looking back at well over sixty years on the water, Captain Hal and Captain Bob are still learning. Sharing some of the stories and lessons that they learned the hard way is what this little book is all about. Regardless of where you are on the boating experience curve, our objective is to cull from our real-life experiences stories that provide a greater understanding of the challenges and complexities of operating a watercraft, and to help you, our readers, anticipate and prepare for the possible outcomes of your actions, or inactions, while on the water. Our goal is to provide memorable stories that will stay with you, thereby helping you become ever more skilled and safety conscious captains.

We would like to thank all those who have provided grist for our mill, the charter captains we have fished with, the places we have traveled, friends with like interests, and especially Captain Keith and the crew from Rescue Boat, who provided Hal with the opportunity to experience these adventures, and Captain Earl, an outstanding charter captain and a wonderful individual who Bob puts at the top of his list of good people. You will come to know these and other characters as the stories evolve.

Captain Hal and Captain Bob admit that we boaters are a funny lot, free spirits to be sure, we love being on and around the water whether under sail or power. We each have our own preferences, our own boating strengths and yes, weaknesses. We run boats of all sizes, types, speeds and costs, often in all kinds of weather, in all sorts of places, from bays and inlets to the great seas of the world...for better or for worse. When underway we each assume the mantle of command by which regardless of our level of formal or informal preparation, *we become singularly responsible for the safety and wellbeing of our vessel and all who sail aboard her.*

Each story has a lesson to share. You may or may not have experienced similar situations...yet. All episodes are based on real events but as the saying goes: Names, places, and some circumstances may have been changed to protect the identity of those involved, herein presumed to be innocent. Lessons may be subtle, and what we each take away from them will likely be a little different. All that said, draw up a chair, sit down, relax, and...

Welcome Aboard!

Part 1
Getting Started

Episode 1

Captain's Log: *Medical Mayday*

Captain Hal Records

In Episode 1 you come aboard a rescue boat with us for the first time as we encounter two incidents of "medical Mayday," The first, "Boom Crash," is about every sailor's nightmare of being hit in the head by a swinging boom, and the second, "Heart Attack," deals with medical emergencies while boating. As our little collection of short stories evolves, you will join us for many adventures. You will come to know our crew, our boats, and our life on the water. Some stories are fun and funny, some are serious and sad, and although names and places may be changed, all are based on real life incidents that we hope you will enjoy and learn from.

Medical Mayday #1. Boom Crash. It is a crisp October Tuesday on Narragansett Bay, the sky is a brilliant blue and the wind is clocking 20 to 25 miles per hour. A great time for an experienced sailor and his wife to end their season with a brisk day on their 39-foot sloop as they sail her to the shipyard for a winter haul-out. The mainsail is trimmed to take full advantage of the wind, and the ride is exhilarating! Unfortunately, these trips do not always end well. In my years as a rescue boat captain I have seen what can go wrong, and more importantly, how many of the problems can be prevented.

I had just hooked up to and was underway with a disabled and stranded power boat in tow, when a frantic message came over Channel 16 on the VHF radio: "Help me, help me, my husband is injured!" Earlier in the season there would have been several responses from area boaters offering their assistance, but today, for whatever reason, there was just silence. The call came again, "Help me, help me."

Hearing no response to the frantic call I keyed my radio, "This is Rescue Boat *Alpha*. What is your situation?"

1

Rescue Boat

The response came immediately: "While coming about my husband, John was hit in the head by the boom and is on the deck and not moving."

I responded, "What is your location?"

She quickly answered, "We are drifting under the center span of the Mount Hope Bridge."

Standard radio procedure in an emergency is to put out a Mayday, and I told her to do this. Her response: "What is a Mayday?"

Knowing time was of the essence, I intervened and called. "Mayday, Mayday this is Rescue Boat *Alpha*. Sailing vessel adrift and located near Mount Hope Bridge in need of immediate medical assistance."

Epilogue: Mayday #1. Boom Crash. The Coast Guard and local law enforcement responded to the Mayday call and transported unconscious Captain John to an emergency vehicle waiting at a nearby launch ramp. As I passed by that ramp with my disabled vessel still in tow, I could see the flashing blue lights of the harbormaster's boat at the dock and the flashing red lights of the ambulance on shore. I did not learn John's fate, but I hope he was treated successfully and lived to sail again.

Neither did I learn how the stricken sailboat was returned to safe harbor. It was evident that no one on board at the time would have been able to do this. Occasionally a harbormaster may assist with this, or a rescue boat service may be contacted to do so.

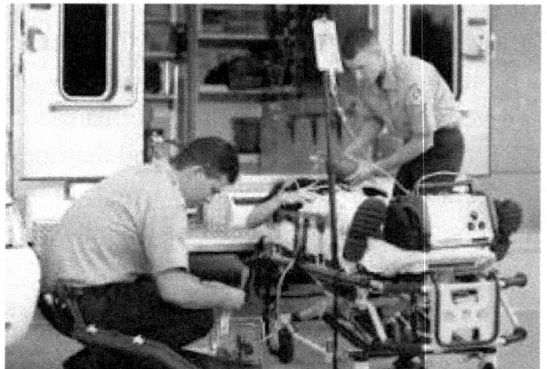

Safety tip: It is important for crew members and passengers on a vessel to know what to do in the event of an emergency. Most captains show crew and guests where the lifejackets and fire extinguishers are, but <u>may be lax in explaining emergency procedures</u> such as how to use a VHF radio. Radio use is important because unlike cellphones that go to one specific place or person, even with 911 calls, a marine radio transmission goes to every boat in the area that has a radio turned on and is tuned to Channel 16. (Although seldom treated as such by the average boater, Channel 16 is a designated hailing channel, which means that as soon as you make contact with your desired party/vessel you should switch to and answer on a different channel/frequency such as 5 or 9. We suggest that you take a moment right now to look up the preferred or designated use for each channel on your VHF.) Hence, a radio transmission is more likely to provide an immediate response from someone on a boat and hopefully much nearer to you than any official rescue vessel. The standard call for help should be: "MAYDAY, MAYDAY, MAYDAY. This is 'VESSEL NAME,'" then state the nature of the emergency and your location.

Managing a vessel in distress: When a captain is incapacitated, and those on board are clueless as to what to do, _everyone on the vessel is exposed to danger_. This is especially true in a sailboat cruising under sail because it cannot be stopped by simply putting it in neutral or turning off the engine. Sails must be luffed, reduced, or even taken down, and the engine started, all the while addressing the emergency or caring for the injured.

An ounce of prevention is worth a pound of cure: A captain should always be sure that there is someone aboard who is sufficiently trained in boat operation (sail or power) so they will be able to manage the vessel in an emergency if the captain is incapacitated, at least until help arrives. They should also understand radio operation well enough to call a Mayday. This training must be done prior to, or at the very beginning of, a cruise. Once disaster strikes it is often too late.

Medical Mayday #2. Heart Attack. It was an early mid-July morning and I was just arriving at Rescue Boat base with my morning Dunkin' coffee in hand when the "near side" VHF sounded with "Mayday, Mayday. My husband is sick." I knew the caller, let's call her Meg, was close based on the volume and clarity of her voice on the radio.

Rescue Boat

As is almost always the case, Coast Guard Sector responded immediately with the critical questions. "What is the nature of your emergency?"

"My husband is not breathing."

"Where are you?"

"Sheep Pen Cove near Patience Island."

"How many persons on board?"

"Two."

"What is the name, make, and size of your boat?"

"A 28-foot Formula, and her name is *Runaway*."

The Coast Guard dispatched a boat from their nearest station and the radio crackled with acknowledgements from the local harbormaster, a fire boat, and a state police boat, all underway to Hogs Pen Cove. Commercial towing and salvage companies do not provide EMT services but rather deal primarily with boat towing, ungroundings, dewaterings, and salvage of sunken and damaged vessels, but we can and often do provide communication and rapid transport in emergency situations. Hence, I went down to the docks, started up Rescue Boat *Phoenix*, the 23-foot RIB, turned on her red and yellow strobe lights, and hastily departed the harbor.

As I arrived on scene, a state police boat was tied to the port side of Meg's boat and the harbormaster's boat tied to the other side. A stretcher was being transferred from Meg's boat to the police boat and although I did not know it at the time, Meg went with her husband on the police boat. Since that left no one on the 28-foot Formula, the harbormaster asked me to tow the boat back to Rescue Boat base pending further instruction.

I pulled alongside the boat, secured my tow hawser to its bow, hauled in and stowed its anchor, and proceeded out of the cove at low speed. Before 20 minutes had passed, I could see flashing blue lights and an environmental police boat approaching my starboard side at a rapid speed. An armed officer standing in the bow ordered me to "heave to" for boarding, which of course I did. They asked me where I was taking the boat and who authorized me to tow it, which I told them. Next, they boarded the formula and spent about 30 minutes doing a thorough search of the vessel, after which they said, "Thank you," and departed as quickly as they had arrived.

Until now I had surmised the medical emergency was a heart attack or stroke, and had learned the patient was a young man in his middle thirties. Having been stopped for a search of Meg's boat, I was beginning to think maybe there was an overdose or some drug involvement.

Epilogue: Mayday #2. Heart Attack. The next day, a boat hauling company hired by Meg came to our marina, loaded the Formula onto a trailer, and took it away. As it turns out there were no drugs involved, and sadly Meg's husband had died from a heart attack before they were able to get him ashore to a hospital.

Episode 2

Captain's Log: *Pending Weather*

Captain Hal Records

In this episode we get a better sense of how rescue boat services operate as we tell the story of a night rescue in a thunderstorm using radio dialogue of what goes on in the pilot house of a rescue boat during a rescue operation. We have concentrated on the most relevant and important radio transmissions, but some transmissions have been left out of the dialogue in the interest of keeping the story moving along and keeping you, the reader, engaged.

20:57 hours, 27 June, Dispatch Office. Mark, a fellow captain at our Rescue Boat office and a reserve Air National Guard officer, had just returned from a run when the landline tone sounded, and its video screen indicated "wireless caller," which usually means a distress call. We always wait and pick up on the second ring to be certain a connection is made. Mark picks up the phone and voices his greeting: "Rescue Boat Dispatch, may I help you?"

A young male caller states that he needs assistance.

Mark faithfully follows procedure and begins to ask and record answers to the relevant questions. "What is the nature of your problem and are you in danger?"

The caller responded, "My engine is broken down and will not start. We are out of the channel and ok."

6

Getting Started

The questions continue: "What is the description of your boat? What color is the boat? How many people are on board? Where do you need to be towed to? What is your name? What is your cellphone number? Are you a Rescue Boat member? Do you have a marine radio aboard?" Finally, the most important question: "Where are you located?"

The caller responds—let's call him Captain Broken Down Dave. "We were fishing near the lighthouse at Bold Point in the Providence River and drifted inboard of the lighthouse where we are anchored near the rocks in shallow water."

Mark responds, "Ok Captain, we will get a boat underway; it should be there in about 30 minutes."

I had just returned from a short run and was enjoying a leisurely cup of too strong coffee when Mark calls out, "Hey Hank, your turn. Here's the info on your caller. You may want to move right along if this radar weather picture is correct." We switch on the NOAA radar to see what looks to be massive thunderstorms moving up from New York and presently covering Eastern Long Island Sound. The photo shows part of the Rescue Boat Dispatch Office. Please note high tech gear including computers with electronic maps, charts, radar, high and low side VHF radios, and best of all, the fishing pole standing in left corner.

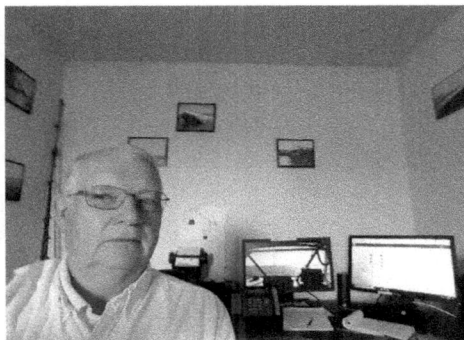

The marine weather forecast is not good. The present light fog is supposed to get heavier and then become interspersed with thunderstorms after 22:00 hours. (10:00 p.m. for you landlubbers.) Rescue operations are always more challenging when certain conditions are present including: 1) darkness and limited visibility when attempting to locate, approach, and hook up a towline; 2) weather fronts that bring fog, rain, and wind which, in addition to limiting vision, makes the approach and hookup much more challenging for the rescue boat captain; 3) uncertain water depth, hazards, and obstructions near and around the disabled vessel; and 4) the condition of the disabled vessel including is the anchor holding, are they taking on water, is there injury of anyone aboard, and is there a clear path out to open water once the towline is attached. When you have two or more of these conditions at the same time, the rescue stress and danger level can elevate very quickly.

21:10 hours, 27 June, Aboard Rescue Boat **Phoenix.** I wasted no time grabbing my go bag (rescue boat captains carry a backpack or canvas bag usually containing water, some sort of food, flashlight, rain gear, hand compass, and other items needed for voyages of unknown duration) and a plastic-enclosed clipboard containing the service order, then headed down to the dock. *Phoenix* is the boat for this run. She is an ex-Coast Guard work boat, a welded aluminum RIB, 26 feet long overall with a pair of 175 Suzuki four-stroke outboard engines mounted on a Gill bracket. She is quick, quiet, highly maneuverable, has long legs (is very fuel efficient) and has remarkable torque and towing power. Two other towboats, *Alert* and *Resilient*, lay quietly against their floating piers.

I don the inflatable life vest draped over the console. By the way, a lifejacket is required to be worn by every person aboard a rescue boat. No exceptions. You would be surprised by how many disabled vessels have five people on board and only four lifejackets! The rescue boats always carry spares to ensure passenger safety during the rescue operation.

As I turn the ignition keys the stern mounted engines immediately come to life, and I can hear the engine cooling water streams as they splash into the bay. The VHF radios automatically switch on and quickly light up the screens, followed by the GPS and the radar units coming online. I stow my go bag and clipboard in the console, release the lines and get underway. As I clear the docks and move into the narrow channel, I flip the switch to activate the flashing red and yellow strobe lights mounted on the cabin top. We activate the strobes when on the way to distress calls and while towing and assisting the craft in need, but we turn them off for the run home. The primary purpose of the strobe lights is to warn other mariners that there is some sort of emergency, and we are responding at the best possible safe speed to aid a mariner in distress, and if towing we have limited maneuverability. The message to all boat operators is to stay clear and out of our way.

Getting Started

Safety Tip: Always be aware and cautious of weather and sea conditions. In this instance, the bay is flat calm, at least for the moment. The air is heavy, visibility is restricted by patches of fog, and night is falling. Leaving the dock on a rescue run always imparts a twinge of excitement...and reticence. Perhaps it is because of what we do. We go when everyone else is either in port or headed for port. Our rescue runs vary from very short, perhaps an hour or two, to day-long or night-long adventures. Our work shifts have starting times, but not ending times. This is because it is much quicker, more efficient, and less expensive for those rescue boats already closest to a vessel in distress to respond, regardless of how long that rescue boat and her captain may have been at sea. The binding constraint to this being the fuel status of the rescue boat. On many occasions I have used the fuel in portable cans that we carry for assisting others just to get back to home port or to the nearest fuel dock after a long and arduous rescue operation.

Captain's Log: 21:35 hours, 27 June, at Oxen Point Light.

It is beautiful out here. The wake stretches out flat and straight behind the boat. Not many boaters out here this evening, at least not many smart ones given the impending weather. My plan is to move quickly around Conimicut Point and into the Providence River, for what will hopefully (always hopefully) be a quick find, and an easy tow to East Providence, giving me enough time to get back to base before the storm arrives. I lean on the throttle and make 30 knots by the time I exit the channel. I need to cover as much distance as possible before darkness and fog seriously impedes progress.

It is nearly dark, and I can see a small white light blinking on and off near the base of the lighthouse, most likely my target. Lights on the waterway are extremely helpful to navigation at night, and light colors and placement have very specific meanings for mariners. White is ordinarily a stern or masthead light, but in this case evidently it is a hand-held flashlight being used to signal me. The vessel in distress is anchored on what appears to be a very short, nearly vertical rode (the anchor line), and is located precipitously close to the giant rocks at the base of the lighthouse. My *"little voice"* says shallow water and I reduce speed to about one knot, just enough to maintain steerage, and operate the hydraulic tilt control to lift my engines out of the water as much as possible while still keeping their water pumps below the surface and enough of the prop in the water to provide propulsion. I am greeted by two young men and two boys who are evidently incredibly pleased at the idea of getting back home safely. Their fishing gear is packed up, they all look a little stressed, and they are smiling and anxious to haul their anchor. I introduce myself, "Hi, my name is Hank, what are your names?"

They respond in sequence, "Bill and this is my boat."

"Jack and these are my boys Sandy and Sam."

As I clip the tow hawser onto the bow ring of their boat, and they haul the anchor which appears to be down only about six feet, we hear a rumble of thunder in the distance. I instruct everyone aboard to be sure their life vest is secure and be prepared to see some changes in the weather as we start our return run. "If you have raingear aboard, get it out and put it on or keep it nearby so you can put it on if we encounter thunderstorms."

Epilogue: 22:15 hours, 27 June, Bold Point Launch Ramp, East Providence

After a brief tow I nudged the towboat alongside the dock with my tow sandwiched safely between me and the dock at the launch ramp. I hold the two boats in position with my engines until Bill has secured his boat to the dock. We hear yet another roll of thunder and the fog has become heavier. I can barely see the launch ramp, which is only a few feet away. I switch on my deck lights and we are suddenly standing in a bright glow. I ask Bill to sign the tow service form, no charge since he is a member, and he thanks me profusely for the quick service. Jack and the two boys have already disappeared up the dock toward their truck. I bid Bill a good evening, turn off the deck lights and the strobe lights, and slip out into the now nearly invisible channel. The run home will be at a safe speed and on instruments. Little did I know what was about to happen.

Uh Oh: 22:30 hours, 27 June, Bold Point, bound for Conimicut Light.

I grab the VHF microphone and key Channel 16 to send, "Rescue Boat Dispatch, Rescue Boat Dispatch. Rescue Boat *Phoenix*. RTB."

Getting Started

(Return To Base is the message we send when clear of our current assist, and on the way home, or ready for another assignment.)

I hear Mark's voice, a welcome sound on this now pitch-dark foggy night with a light rain starting to fall, but I do not get the expected response, "Roger *Phoenix* RTB." What I did get was, "Switch and answer 07." My heart started to race, as the dread I felt earlier returned. Something was surely coming down. As one rescue mission continues into another, this episode continues into another, Episode 3: "Trouble at Fogland Point."

Episode 3

Captain's Log: *Trouble at Flogland Point*

Captain Hal Records

In Episode 2, "Pending Weather," Captain Hal told the story of a late evening rescue of four fishermen in the face of deteriorating weather conditions. This episode, "Trouble at Fogland Point," picks up where that story leaves off and we again join him on Rescue Boat *Phoenix*, the 26-foot RIB.

The sun had dipped below the horizon and I was nearing the end of my shift. So far, the day had been filled with routine calls, nothing exciting but certainly important to the boat owners and captains who needed assistance. I had just completed towing a 23-foot Wellcraft center console experiencing engine problems to where their trailer was parked at the Bold Point Ramp in the Providence River. The fog was beginning to roll in, so I was keeping one eye on my GPS and the other on the pulsing radar screen as I left the dock and picked my way south between the channel markers. Visibility was becoming an issue, and I wanted to get back into open water as quickly as possible. I was about to check in with Rescue Boat Dispatch when my VHF radio sounded.

On dispatch I heard Captain Mark's steady voice, "Rescue Boat *Phoenix*, Rescue Boat Dispatch, we have a 35-foot sailing vessel aground on the rocks south of Fogland Point in the Sakonnet River. The Coast Guard is on scene and will free the vessel from the rocks. There is a storm approaching and the weather is closing in fast. Can you take this call for assistance since you are the closest to their location?"

My mind was racing, yeah right, closest to it but still 23 nautical miles away. I responded "Mark, I can make the run and will tow them back to the boat basin in Tiverton Harbor. I have plenty of fuel, but can make only 12 knots in this pea soup fog. ETA to vessel in distress is two hours at current speed."

Mark responded, "Roger that, but you will break out of your current weather south of Prudence Island and should then be able to make better time. You will be in better visibility in 10 minutes."

"Roger that. Rescue Boat *Phoenix* standing by Channel 16, 07." I reached down and switched on my flashing red and yellow emergency strobe lights and immediately noticed that they cast an eerie shadow in the fog.

Log Entry: 22:45 hours, 27 June, Passing Prudence Island, Bound for the Mount Hope Bridge and the Sakonnet River.
"Rescue Boat Dispatch, Rescue Boat Dispatch, Rescue Boat *Phoenix*."

"Rescue Boat *Phoenix*, Rescue Boat Dispatch, switch and answer Channel 07."

"Mark, you should be a weatherman, I just cleared the rain and fog, the sea conditions are flat and calm, and I am now making 35 knots. Revised ETA on site is 23:45 hours."

"Hank good going, I thought it would get better. Coast Guard has the boat off the rocks and will stand by until you arrive. Good luck. Keep me posted." As I switched back to Channel 16 and returned the microphone to its overhead clip, I could again hear the rumble of thunder over the now high-pitched throbbing of my engines. Speed at night on the water can be both exhilarating and scary at the same time. My wake formed a sharp vee behind the boat and was nearly flat at this speed. Under these conditions and at this speed, there is little danger of my falling asleep at the helm while running with such a limited visibility window!

23:15 hours, 27 June, Approaching Sakonnet River Bridge headed 180 degrees, bound for Fogland Point. As I approached the Sakonnet River Bridge I could see

that something was going on, there were blue strobe lights flashing under the center span. When I slowed to pass under the bridge, I saw a Coast Guard 34-foot SAFE boat, and the crew was hailing me. As I approached, they said they had just come from Fogland Point and had pulled the sailboat off the rocks. They told me she had not been holed by by being on the rocks, was not taking on water, and was safely anchored just off the shoreline. Her crew of five was safe and seemed calm, but her engine had failed and there was, no wind with which they could sail back to port; meanwhile, the storm front was rapidly approaching. Overall, a welcome report. They said getting her to safe harbor was now up to me and that they were on their way to yet another vessel in distress. They headed north and I south.

23:45 hours, 27 June. I again powered up and made good time until about one mile north of my target, where the fog bank made it almost impossible to see my forward tow post only about eight feet in front of the pilothouse window. This was the epic "pea soup" fog. Back to instruments and about eight knots of speed. Fortunately, I could see the distressed vessel on my Furuno radar and combined with a GPS was able to reach them without incident. Their anchor and running lights showed as dull glows in the fog as I came alongside. We exchanged greetings and I passed them a tow bridle with a tow hawser attached. Let's call the captain, Rob. Rob ran the bridle outboard of their bow rail and attached an eye to each of his two forward cleats.

I described the likely situation of the trip back north up the Sakonnet River to their marina in Tiverton. We would try to maintain six to seven knots of speed, would tow them  about 50 yards astern, and we would both stay on VHF Channel 7 for communications. I told Rob he needed to keep someone on the helm at all times, and to steer to the center of my wake if they could see it. If caught by a severe thunderstorm, I would shorten the hawser and hold us both bow to the wind until the worst of the storm had passed.

01:45 hours, 28 June. The tow back was slow and relatively uneventful, except for the ever closer and louder rumbles of thunder. Most of the time I was unable to see the sailboat behind me due to the fog, and periodically gave the hawser a tug with my hand just to be sure she was still there. I spoke with Rob on the VHF as we approached their harbor. As soon I passed through the opening to Tiverton Harbor at the old stone bridge, I stopped, put the towboat in neutral, and allowed Rob's boat to glide up on my starboard side while hauling in, thereby shortening the tow hawser. The big sailboat glided up beside me like a ghost in the night until I was able to lash her port hip to the starboard side of the towboat. This is standard procedure for maneuvering a tow in the tight spaces of a harbor and into a dock or slip. With visibility so low, I asked Rob to position his crew along the length of his boat and alert me if we were too close to anything. We were picking our way carefully through the foggy anchorage filled with boats when all hell broke loose. Fortunately we were very close to his dock and just as I nudged them against their pier, lightning flashed, thunder crashed, and rain came down like we were standing directly under a fire hose. Rob and his crew quickly secured their boat to the pier. I told Rob we would deal with paperwork another day, and he scurried up the dock with his crew to a waiting knot of people clustered under umbrellas. Their loved ones had been worried and were glad to see them safely home.

I piled the tow hawser and bridle unceremoniously on my aft deck, retrieved the lines holding me to Rob's boat, and slowly picked my way to a close by marina where my friend Don kept his 31-foot Cabo sport fisherman. By now lightning made it look like daylight, rain was literally dancing off the surface of the harbor and pounding on my aluminum hull and pilot house. It was a little scary but also somehow beautiful. Now comes decision time, should I hide out until the storm passes or fight the weather and attempt to return to my home port an hour away? I made the safer choice, tied the towboat to the dock, and climbed aboard Don's boat, which was fiberglass and not metal like Rescue Boat *Phoenix*, providing some protection from the ever-present lightening.

Rescue Boat

02:45 hours, 28 June. Dispatch radioed that there would very soon be a break in the storms, and I had about 60 minutes to get back to base before the next round rolled in. I took advantage of the brief weather window, left the shelter of my friend's marina, put the hammers down and pulled the rescue boat up to our home dock exactly one hour later. The boss, Captain Keith, stood on the dock awaiting my arrival. He had heard our radio exchanges on the VHF located in his home and made his way back to base in the middle of the night, relieving Captain Mark. He helped me secure the boat and then made a statement I have never forgotten: "Being a rescue boat captain is not for everyone!" (No joke, Charlie Brown)

Epilogue. Simply stated, it is never over until it is over when you are on the water. Yes, that night I was able to help a vessel needing assistance. I was in a very seaworthy but open metal RIB boat, on a turbulent expanse of water in a severe thunderstorm. Life on the water is all about assessing risk and making smart decisions rather than emotional ones. Is it worth it to risk the boat, perhaps even my life, to immediately get back to my home dock? Only the captain can decide, and when dealing with weather, you can never be sure of the intensity or duration of a storm on the water. Usually the conservative decision is the better one; it will allow you to survive to fight again another day. Even if you need to "borrow" someone's dock or mooring and tie up until the storm passes.

Episode 4

Captain's Log: *Alcohol and Water Don't Mix*

Captain Robert Behling and Captain Hal Records

In this episode, "Alcohol and Water Don't Mix," Captain Bob and Captain Hal relate two stories about what can happen when boaters do mix alcohol and water. We call the first story "Dumb and Dumber," and the second, "How Did We Get Home?" The theme of both stories is that alcohol and water do not mix, and we trust that neither of these incidents were you.

Captain Bob's words of wisdom*: Have you ever wondered why, when you buy a case of bottled drinking water there is an expiration date? Does water spoil? Wear out? Go bad? Or might your case of water include water molecules from Cleopatra's bath water, Lewis and Clark's expedition down the Columbia River to the Pacific, or even the Pacific itself?*

Background. A trip to a marina or launching ramp anywhere in the United States will find boaters loading up for a day on the water, usually with a cooler nestled among their fishing and swimming gear. The cooler could contain bottled water or soda, but it probably also includes some beer. Nothing beats a cold beer on a hot day, especially on the water. Beer contains alcohol, and in small doses it is not likely to impair judgement or coordination. Unfortunately, small doses may be followed by larger doses, and the resulting degradation of function. Operating a boat is no different from operating a motor vehicle and being impaired from ingesting alcohol clouds judgment, impairs vision, and generally puts the boat operator, his or her passengers, and others on the water at risk.

Rescue Boat

Captain's Log. Dumb and Dumber: While waiting to launch and enjoy a day of fishing on Cape Cod, I saw two enthusiastic boaters, let's call them Dumb and Dumber, load their boat with fishing gear and two heavy coolers. I had suspicions of what the coolers may have contained but at that point it was none of my business.

As I was securing my trailer, I overheard Dumb say to Dumber, "Are you sure we have enough beer in the cooler?"

Dumber responded, "I put two cases and a bag of ice in the coolers; that should hold us for the day." Shaking my head at their choice of hydration for the day, I launched my boat when the ramp was free and went on my merry way. A day on the water can be relaxing and fishing often brings added excitement from "catching the big one!" I did find fish, but the big one eluded me. I returned to the ramp and loaded my boat on my trailer around suppertime, cleaned some fish and headed home. The boat with the two heavy coolers had not yet returned. Later I learned of Dumb and Dumber's fate.

Situation: It was very hot on the water, and dehydration is always a possibility. Having a few beers keeps you hydrated, but also loads your system with alcohol. Fishing can be ok, and at times can be boring, so as the afternoon progresses the trip often becomes more social, sitting around and telling stories while waiting for a tight line. Good friends, having a good time on the water, how great is that?

By the time the coolers were emptied dusk was setting in, and the fishermen realized they needed to get back to the dock before dark. They had a compass but no charts, had not paid attention to their location as they moved the boat looking for fish, and while they had a general idea of the direction of the landing ramp, they were not sure how far they needed to go. Pull the anchor, secure the fishing equipment, start the engine and head for home! Because it was getting dark, speed was essential to get to the landing before dark. *With impaired judgment, speed magnifies the opportunity for bad things to happen*.

Their repositioning the boat during the day put a reef between them and the boat ramp, and because they were looking for good fishing spots, they did not pay much attention during their boat movements. Knowing the ramp should be due east, the captain put on maximum power and headed in a straight line for home. Because of the low light and the difficulty seeing marking and danger buoys on the reef, because of the consumption of lots of beer, and because they were not sure exactly where they were, disaster happened. Traveling at about 30 knots per hour they impacted the reef, tore open the bottom of their boat, and immediately took on water. They had lifejackets on board but were not wearing them. They had signaling flares, but they were under water. They were in big trouble.

Epilogue "Dumb and Dumber." Fortunately, the reef created a shallow water situation, and while the boat took on water and started sinking, it eventually came to rest on the reef. Dumb and Dumber were banged around upon impact, being thrown against the boat console with some force. Neither was knocked out, nor were they thrown out of the boat. The boat was not operable, so they were stuck on the reef until help came, and with no running lights operating, that probably would not be until morning. They were in for a wet and cold night. Their families had a general idea of where they planned to fish but were short on specifics. Dumb and Dumber had not filed a float plan. Their wives, Sally and Jane, talked with each other, then they called the Coast Guard. They were told to be patient and see if Dumb and Dumber return in the next several hours. By dawn it was clear that they were in trouble, so a search was initiated.

Shortly after dawn an early fisherman passed near enough to the reef to see the people in distress and radioed the Coast Guard their position. On scene the Coast Guard 34-foot RIB extracted the stranded people who were cold and wet but otherwise ok. They contacted a rescue boat service to salvage and remove the boat from the reef before more fuel was spilled. When there is a pollution hazard on the water, salvage is out of the hands of the vessel owner; the Coast Guard has a mandate to protect the water quality from pollution. The vessel owner will be charged for the salvage service, however, so once again there may be an incentive to investigate both rescue boat services and hull insurance. After taking the stranded fishermen Dumb and Dumber aboard, the search was terminated by the Coast Guard who broadcast the message "Vessel Assisted" on VHF Channel 16.

The hull of the fishing boat took a pretty good hit when it impacted the reef, and salvage was not an easy operation. Fortunately, the tide was ebbing, and the rescue boat service was able to secure several inflatable devices to the hull, and as the tide came in the severely damaged hull was floated off the reef. The trip back to the marina was slow, as the bottom was destroyed. The boat was about half full of water and the damaged hull was causing drag on the tow. The inflatables kept it afloat, but speed was very slow. Rescue boat services on salvage calls generally charge a base call charge, and then add charges for time to completion of the salvage operation. In this case it took two hours to secure the inflatables, and four hours to tow the hull back to the marina. The hull was not repairable, so it was a total loss. The salvage operation came to four figures, and Dumb and Dumber found that they had a very expensive fishing trip that day.

Captain's Log. 19:00 hours 3 July. "How did we get home?" It had been a very busy day and Captain Hank had just finished refueling Rescue Boat *Thor*, a 26-foot center console, step hull, Bluefin boat with a pair of vintage Mercury Optimax engines mounted on an Armstrong bracket. Although she was the only one of the five boat fleet still running two stroke engines, she was the fastest and topped out at a little over 41 knots. (about 50 miles per hour for you landlubbers). This was Fourth of July Eve, so we knew it would be a long day and true to form, the VHF sounded even before I could get off the boat to stretch my legs. Dispatch had a 22-foot Regal inboard-outboard broken down near the "milk bottle" in the Providence River about 30 minutes away. The milk bottle is a lighthouse-like structure built in the river just outside the channel that, you guessed it, looks a lot like a giant milk bottle.

Captain's Log. 19:30 hours 3 July, Providence River. The boat was anchored, or at least sort of anchored, because the anchor line was straight up down in about 15 feet of water when I arrived. The river was calm and there was some boat traffic moving by at a safe distance. I could see three people in the boat. A young woman, let's call her Jane, was at the helm seat and had made the VHF call for assistance. There was a young man sitting in the copilot seat and another in the port jump seat at the stern. Both were either sound asleep or passed out and did not wake as I came alongside. Jane was coherent, but I think feeling no pain. She said it was her boat and the only thing she needed was fuel so she could continue on her way.

The fuel fill was on the transom directly behind the port jump seat, and her passenger, let's call him John, did not respond when I asked him to move, so I literally lifted and dragged him to the starboard jump seat. Next, I emptied a red five-gallon tank of gas into the fuel fill and asked Jane to start the engine, which she did.

Captain's Log. 20:00 hours 3 July, Providence River. So far, so good. I asked Jane where she was headed and she said back to her dock in Warwick Cove which was to the south and the general direction that I would be traveling back to base, so I asked her to follow me at least as far as the entrance to her harbor. Well, Jane hauled her anchor and got underway, but she would be close astern, then fall back, then be off to port, then off to starboard. I had clearly made a mistake in asking her to drive so I contacted her by cellphone and asked to her to heave to so that I could tow her home. She seemed relieved and so was I. I hooked the hawser snap to the bow eye of her boat and proceeded to tow her back.

Captain's Log. 20:30 hours 3 July, Warwick Cove Harbor. Upon arrival in the harbor she was barely able to tell me which marina and slip were hers and she was unable to assist with docking or line handling. Fortunately, the slip next to hers was vacant so that I was able to nudge both *Thor* and Jane's boat into the slip. I climbed across her boat, tied it to the dock, and left Jane with a tow receipt and not a bill since as a member there was no charge for the service.

Epilogue. "How did we get home?" As I released *Thor's* dock lines from Jane's boat, she was sound asleep. John and his companion never did wake up. I am quite sure that by Fourth of July morning when they awoke they would have huge headaches and none of them would remember me or have any idea how they got home. Alcohol and water do not mix; Boating Under the Influence (BUI) is as dangerous as Driving Under the Influence (DUI). Jane and her friends were lucky, if not smart. No one drowned or was injured, and they were safely towed home by rescue boat. Had it been the Coast Guard or a local harbormaster that towed them in, they would have been charged with Boating Under the Influence and awakened in jail.

Episode 5

Captain's Log: *Don't Threaten Me*

Captain Hal Records

Episode 5, "Don't Threaten Me," as told by Captain Hal, reveals a rare kind of character and behavior that none of us ever want to see on the water. It was the kind of rescue that would have been much less stressful if done by a Navy destroyer such as the one pictured in the background here.

It was a sultry August afternoon, the temperature was in the 80s, and there was a great deal of boat traffic moving in and out of the channel into New Harbor on Block Island 14 miles off the coast of Rhode Island. All five area rescue boats had been running since early morning for fuel drops, jump-starts, soft ungroundings (when a boat has run aground, is not damaged, and can be refloated by a single rescue boat and or at a higher tide) and tows back to harbor. Although most boaters are capable, courteous, and understanding, especially when they are in need of assistance, there are also those who become demanding, arrogant, and aggressive. In my years as a rescue boat captain I have developed a sixth sense, a *little voice* that tells me when something is amiss.

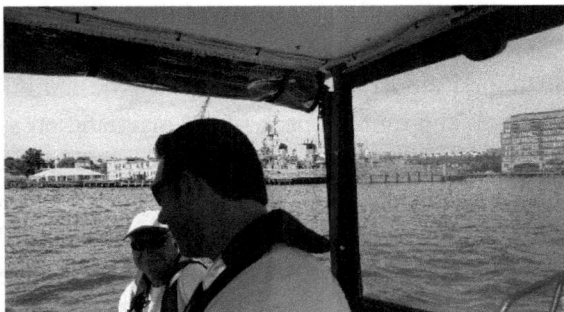

Log entry: I had just completed a tow back to the mainland and refueled the 23-foot Steiger known as Rescue Boat Three, ready and hoping for a little break from the day's hectic pace when I received a call on my cellphone from Keith in Central Dispatch. Captain Keith was our

Rescue Boat

boss and owner of the local rescue boat franchise for which we worked. Captain Keith is a character of the first order, a quietly spoken man, with a heart of gold, and a will of iron. He did many if not most of the overnight rescue runs and we would frequently find him asleep on the futon in the dispatch office when we showed up for the early morning shift. He has run rescue boats for many years, is a first-rate engine mechanic, and knows how to take good care of his customers and crew.

Keith said the new customer was irate in requesting assistance. She and a friend had spent the previous night on a nearby island in their 38-foot Scarab go-fast boat (The kind of boat that could make a quick dash in the dark of night to get out to sea and back to the island before dawn if her crew had a mind to). Let's call the crew Bonnie and Clyde. I am reminded of the rum runners of prohibition times who used fast boats and dark nights to transport alcoholic beverages from ships at sea outside the then three-mile limit into islands, nooks, and crannies all around the coastal United States, thereby eluding federal law enforcement agents who were attempting to interrupt their illegal smuggling activities.

On the Scarab in question, one of the twin engines was reportedly down and inoperable. Bonnie and Clyde did not want to attempt leaving the dock and running back to the mainland on a single engine without assistance. As always, I telephoned the vessel in distress as soon as I cleared the breakwater to see if they were ok, and to give them my ETA at their location. The customary customer response to these calls was relief and yes, even a bit of thankfulness in knowing that help was on the way within a now defined time period. But Bonnie was very curt, and she wanted to know exactly why it would take me half an hour to cover the 20-mile run to the island in moderate four-foot seas. *Hello little voice.*

Curious Situation: Upon arrival at the island and alongside their boat, both Bonnie and Clyde were hostile to me. They did not want to hear that with one of their oversized inboard engines fully operational I could escort them out of the harbor and beyond the Coast Guard station, after which they could proceed on their own power back to port. They insisted that I put them on the hip, in a side by side towing position normally used when the vessel being towed has no engine power at all, at least until we were beyond the Coast Guard station. *Hello little voice.*

Getting Started

This I did, and at the same time attached a tow hawser and bridle to Bonnie and Clyde's bow in the unlikely event the second engine failed and they really did need to be towed once we were in the open sea outside the channel.

We then got underway, weaving through a large and busy anchorage filled with all manner of sail and power boats, both on moorings and in motion. As we approached the narrow exit channel which is bordered closely on both sides by rock seawalls and bustling with boat traffic, we headed into rolling four-foot swells. I listened to the _little voice_ telling me something was not right and used my cellphone to call Central Dispatch. This is not normal procedure, but as a safety precaution I put my phone on speaker, positioned it on the helm, and asked Captain Keith to stand by in case I needed assistance. The Scarab was running well with one engine, and in fact unbeknownst to Bonnie and Clyde, my engines were both in neutral. When I told Captain Clyde we were clear enough beyond the narrow channel and to release the lines holding us side by side he refused. (Please bear in mind the rescue boat is 23 feet long with a pair of 140 hp outboard engines. The Scarab 38-footer had two 400-plus horsepower engines, even one of which could overpower the rescue boat with ease. The Scarab dwarfed the rescue boat in every sense.) Clyde said in a loud voice, "If you attempt to release the lines, I will steer your boat into the seawall, crush it, and kill you." Yeah, _little voice_, yeah cellphone still on speaker.

With my cellphone still on speaker, I told Captain Clyde that we could not keep the two boats lashed together in the open sea any longer and we needed to separate them now. I waited what seemed like way too long and until well clear of the channel and seawall, before Captain Clyde finally released the lines tying the two boats closely together. As I moved Rescue Three away from his side and into a towing position forward of him, my starboard engine failed. I again told him that it was safer and faster for him to simply run the 30 miles or so back to his home port on his single operating engine, especially since I had only one engine running on the towboat. He refused. He continued to refuse until I told him that if he did not release it, I would cut the hawser. He finally released the hawser and I hauled it back into Rescue Three while running parallel to him and about 200 yards off his port side.

Rescue Boat

In the meantime, while all this was going on Captain Clyde had telephoned the Coast Guard and requested a tow, saying that he was stranded and I would not tow him. The Coast Guard called Captain Keith at Rescue Boat Dispatch, and then me for a situation assessment. I told them Captain Clyde was making more speed than I, that sea conditions were relatively calm and that he was in no danger. The Coast Guard did not dispatch a vessel to assist him but did put out a MARB (Marine Assistance Radio Broadcast) on Channel 16 to which another rescue boat company responded. As Bonnie and Clyde made their way around the island and toward the mainland, I stayed at a distance but within sight until the second rescue boat arrived just to be sure they were safe. While shadowing Bonnie and Clyde, Captain Keith said that because my starboard engine restarted easily, and then shut down immediately upon engaging the clutch, the propeller was most likely fouled. As usual he was correct in his diagnosis and as soon as I tilted the engine out of the water and removed a tangled piece of rope from the propeller, the engine ran fine.

Epilogue. To this day I am not sure of Bonnie and Clyde's motivation. I told Captain Keith somewhat unconvincingly that it was no doubt an idle threat to crush my boat and kill me, and then hung up the cellphone. Having heard the conversation, Captain Keith immediately and permanently cancelled that customer's membership, and suggested to Bonnie and Clyde they would be happier if they sold their boat and bought a nice RV.

In retrospect, we are told that Bonnie and Clyde paid a very healthy fee for their unnecessary tow which suggests there may have been some other reason they wanted to be towed past the Coast Guard station, and back to their mainland harbor. What might be that reason? From a distance the Scarab appeared to be a little low on her waterline, like maybe she was carrying a little more than just Bonnie and Clyde. In any event—and fortunately—I was never again asked to respond to a service call from that vessel.

Captain's Note - Protecting Yourself on the Water: The "Don't Threaten Me" story brings to mind the hotly debated topic of having firearms on boats. Handguns are often carried aboard both motor and sailing vessels, perhaps for personal security of the captain and crew. Shotguns and even stainless-steel large caliber weapons designed for use around salt water are used, especially by serious shark fishermen. I have on more than one occasion been tuna fishing and had large sharks 10 or 12 feet long literally tear the entire belly out of a 100-pound tuna that has been hooked, brought alongside, gaffed, and was bleeding profusely into the water while being moved aft toward the tuna door. In this situation a 12-gauge shotgun loaded with buckshot can be held over the gunnel and fired at a range of about two feet from the shark just before he strikes the tuna. The shot will punch a hole in the shark about the size of your fist; the shark will shake his head and swim away, but will not get his tuna dinner. After this, tuna fishermen must move very quickly to get the tuna aboard because sharks do not dine alone. There will be three or more sharks immediately behind the first, and after getting the hooked tuna aboard it is advisable to move your boat two or three miles to a new location to temporarily elude the sharks. Yet I digress—back to the topic at hand, more about firearms and boating.

Many rescue boat captains are off duty or retired police, ex-military, and/or have concealed weapon carry permits. They generally have extensive training in the use of firearms, dealing with dangerous encounters, and staying cool and calm. I am ex-Navy but choose not to carry. I believe that the sight of firearms often causes agitation, which may lead to an escalation of tension and ultimately an unwanted outcome. It is a personal choice, not a mandate. Virtually all rescue boat captains do carry sharp knives to cut away tow ropes and lines in an emergency. Every rescue call is unique, and you never know exactly what you might encounter.

The same holds true for a private citizen responding to a MARB or going to the aid of someone requesting assistance over the marine radio. Being alert to possible danger, being cautious of boaters obviously consuming large amounts of alcohol, being aware that people aboard the boat you are approaching might be armed, and taking care when approaching a vessel asking for assistance are just the smart things to do. It is not recommended that you apply for a carry permit or board your vessel armed, just that you exercise caution when responding to a request for help. Wonderful people enjoy boating, but there are always a few individuals who may be looking for an opportunity to take advantage of an unsuspecting good Samaritan.

Episode 6

Captain's Log: *Out of Fuel*

Captain Robert Behling and Captain Hal Records

In Episode 6, "Out of Fuel," Captain Bob and Captain Hal tell three stories of mariners running out of fuel, the first on an offshore fishing trip, the second on a safely anchored jet ski, and the third on a jet ski lost and adrift at night. Captain Bob knows from experience fishing around the world that the simplest mistakes may cause the greatest problems, and over the years Captain Hal has responded to many calls from mariners stranded and out of fuel.

#1. Offshore Fishing and Out of Fuel. The sun is shining, the sky is blue, and you are ready to gather up the family, jump into your boat, and head for the open water. A perfect day for boating, fishing, and family fun. As you load everyone up you are thinking "It just doesn't get any better than this." Scenes like this are happening every day, especially along the shores of Cape Cod, where there is an abundance of coastline and beautiful boating and fishing water. Unfortunately, these trips do not always end well.

Captain Bob and several others were planning to head for one of their favorite offshore fishing spots on a friend's 23-foot wide beam boat, the perfect offshore fishing platform. The individual assigned to transfer the extra fuel tanks from the pickup truck to the boat after we launched either did not understand or forgot. We all got on board and headed out from our home port into Pleasant Bay, and after passing through the sandbar cut at the Coast Guard station, we entered the Atlantic Ocean.

Rescue Boat

After a 40-minute run we reached our destination off Monomoy Point on the elbow of Cape Cod and began hunting for signs of a school of striped bass. Diving birds, water turbulence, and a congregation of fishing boats often point the way to fish.

The run out exhausted most of the fuel in the tank, so the captain, let's call him Captain Jim, decided to refuel before we started fishing. "John, get the fuel containers and fill the tank," Captain Jim said.

John looked bewildered, and we all looked to each other and said almost in unison, "Where are the fuel containers?" The watercraft had a cuddy cabin, and I thought they might be there, but alas, they were nowhere to be found, forgotten in the back of the truck in the launch parking area. We had nowhere near enough fuel to return to any launch ramp, so Captain Jim radioed the Coast Guard asking for help. Because there was no injury or life-threatening situation, Captain Jim was told to contact a commercial rescue service for assistance.

As soon as the message from Coast Guard Dispatch was completed the radio sprang to life. "Fishing vessel *Cast About*, this is Tom at the Cape Cod Water Taxi service dock. I overheard your conversation with the Coast Guard, and I can provide you with fuel to get you back to the boat ramp. Give me your exact location, and I will head out immediately. The charge will be fifty dollars."

Epilogue: #1 Offshore Fishing and Out of Fuel. At the time Captain Jim did not have rescue insurance, so his options for help were limited. Our fishing trip was in the summer tourist season, so the water taxi service was manned and operating daily. "We are off Monomoy Point. Look for a blue and white vessel."

The water taxi arrived with a fuel container with five gallons of gasoline, but he did not have any two-cycle outboard oil. Because we were running an older Evinrude 115 two-cycle outboard engine we needed to mix the oil with the gas. Fortunately, we scrounged around in the cubby and found an unopened quart of oil tucked away under a bench.

Once refueled and underway, the water taxi followed us to the nearest boat ramp, which was not where we had parked the pickup. Captain Jim had called his wife on his cellphone, and she met us at the dock with the funds to pay for the fuel and gave Jim a ride back to the home launch ramp. Captain Jim retrieved his truck and trailer, returned, and we loaded the boat and headed for home, not looking forward to a fishless dinner that evening. We never even got the chance to wet a line. We later came to understand that the fifty dollar charge was quite reasonable compared to what we would have to pay a rescue boat service. The moral of the story is to always check fuel, safety equipment, bait if going fishing, and battery life for communications equipment before you leave the dock. Once on the water your options are limited when you forget something as important as fuel.

#2. On a Jet Ski and Out of Fuel. In another similar situation, two boaters were stranded on a PWC, let's call them Stan and Tara. The rescue boat operations center had been busy with numerous requests for assistance all morning when we received a radio request from a personal watercraft anchored about 10 miles from the harbor. They were very fortunate to be in water shallow enough to anchor, and they had both an operating cellphone and handheld VHF radio. "We are stranded and out of fuel, and the Coast Guard is unable to provide us with assistance. Can you help us, please?" They had radioed the Coast Guard requesting assistance in returning to the dock as they ran out of fuel.

The Coast Guard inquired about any life-threatening circumstances, and there were none, so they were unable to assist and suggested contacting a commercial rescue boat service. Given the go-ahead by the Stan, the Coast Guard then broadcast a MARB (Marine Assistance Radio Broadcast) over VHF Radio Channel 16 inviting any available assistors to contact the vessel in need. Stan also initiated a radio request for assistance.

Epilogue: #2. On a Jet Ski and Out of Fuel. Our Rescue Boat Service responded to the radio call and we delivered 5 gallons of gas to Stan and Tara. They were charged $365. Stan was in shock! The charge was $15 for the gas, and a one-hour minimum rescue boat charge of $350. Fortunately, Tara had her credit card aboard, so they were able to pay *as expected at the time of service.* Had they been members of the Rescue Boat Service they would have paid only $15 for the fuel instead of the $365 they were charged. Economics lesson 101 - Rescue boat services charge less than $200 per year for membership that usually includes unlimited tows, fuel drops, and battery jumps. So how many times a year would Stan and Tara need to use their rescue boat membership to save money? The moral of the story is, once again, check before leaving the dock. If you leave with a full tank and run out of fuel, obviously you have exceeded the range of your fuel tank, so a wise boater would be aware of their runtime maximum and not exceed it before returning to the home dock.

#3. On a Lost and Out of Fuel Jet Ski. It was the midnight witching hour at 00:01 on July 5. The Fourth of July holiday had been crazy busy, and I was finally headed back to Rescue Boat base after completing six back to back tows. I was again running Rescue Boat *Thor*, the 26-foot Bluefin center console powered with two thirsty Mercury Optimax 150hp outboards. My fuel gauge was bouncing on empty and I was just tying up after what I thought was my last tow of the day to its dock at the Portsmouth Abbey in the East Passage of Narragansett Bay when a young man in his early twenties came running down the ramp to the dock. Let's call him Slim.

Slim was worried because his brother Tom had just telephoned him to say that he was out of fuel and adrift on his jet ski in the bay somewhere north of Conanicut Island when his cellphone failed, probably from a dead battery. Tom was alone on the jet ski. He did not have a VHF radio or an anchor on board, was wearing only a bathing suit and T-shirt, and had left his dock at the Abbey at about 19:00 hours. *Hello little voice.* This could be or become a case of exposure with life-threatening consequences since the temperature at this late hour was now in the low 60s.

Getting Started

Slim asked if he could come aboard and go with me to help find his brother. I gave him an inflatable lifejacket and as we left the Abbey I activated my emergency flashing strobe lights. We headed south into the open bay in the general direction of the Prudence Island T-pier. The light wind was from the south and fog was building, so our rescue plan was to stop just north of the island, listen and call out to him, then repeat this until we found him. My fuel gauge was still bouncing off empty, giving us about 45 minutes of runtime, and I could get another 30 minutes or so by dumping the sole remaining five-gallon reserve can into the main fuel tank.

We ran to our first stop location, shut down the engines and called out across the pitch black water for Tom. Silence. We moved about a mile and repeated the procedure. Silence. By the time we reached our third location the fog was thickening, and *Thor's* red and yellow strobe lights cast an eerie pulsing glow into the dark.

About twenty minutes later, on our fourth stop and call out, we thought we heard a response. I restarted the engines and we moved ever so slowly in the direction of the voice until we spotted Tom. He was clinging to a small line that he had managed to secure to a lobster pot buoy, thereby holding the jet ski in a stationary position. I flipped on *Thor's* deck lights. Slim and I could see that Tom was wet and shivering uncontrollably, yet at the sight of us he broke out in a big smile. I think maybe he was glad to see us!

Slim and I helped him aboard, wrapped him in a blanket, then secured the tow hawser clip to the bow eye of the jet ski. I climbed down onto the jet ski and shut off its water intake valve. This must be done before towing a jet ski, otherwise water will be forced through the intake and into the manifold of the engine, pretty much destroying it.

Epilogue: #3. On a Lost and Out of Fuel Jet Ski. It was 01:00 hours when I returned Slim, Tom, and the jet ski to their dock at the Abbey. They thanked me profusely and as they headed up the ramp to their car, I headed out of the harbor, turned *Thor's* strobe lights off, and set a course for Rescue Base using GPS and radar. About 10 minutes into the foggy run, my starboard engine coughed and shut down. I poured the last five gallons of fuel from the reserve gas can into the very nearly empty 100-gallon fuel tank and made it back to base with the engines practically running on fumes.

Rescue Boat

Keep in mind that a rescue boat captain understands the limitations of his or her watercraft and fuel on board, and there are times when a decision must be made by the captain before responding to a call for help, especially if it involves searching for a mariner in need. Fortunately, in this case the search was not prolonged, and the available fuel was just enough to rescue the individual and return to Rescue Boat base. Had the fuel run out, I would have been the one calling Rescue Boat to bring me more fuel.

Caution: A good rule of thumb for fuel management is to plan for 25 percent to get where you are going, 25 percent to use when you are there, and 25 percent to get back home. The remaining 25 percent is a ready reserve that may be needed due to sea conditions or other unexpected factors.

Boaters need to be aware that these rescue boat companies charge for their services, and, depending on the circumstances, the bill could reach four figures. During the busy boating season when lots of boats are out and about, private parties may offer help, but boaters cannot depend on assistance from others. Requesting fuel can be a problem; many vessels have built in tanks and do not have the option of removing a few gallons to help someone out. Rescue boats carry containers of fuel that can be safely transferred to a vessel, and boaters should always keep safety in mind any time they are dealing with volatile and explosive fuel.

On occasion, when necessary to transfer small quantities of fuel in a heavy sea, the rescue boat will attach a line to a five-gallon gas can and then float it downwind to the vessel needing fuel. Today's safety cans are very difficult to pour in any conditions, let alone rough weather. In the photo at the beginning of this episode, the old-style gas can is on the left and the new style on the right. The old style has a simple screw-on spout and pours easily and quickly with minimum spillage, however *the new style safety spouts designed to prevent spillage almost universally cause spillage.* Any time you are transferring fuel, be sure that no one on the vessel is smoking, and that there are no sources of a spark that could ignite the fuel, such as cellphones.

Safety tip: Most private rescue services offer a subscription or insurance like program where you pay an annual premium and if you

34

have a problem on the water they will assist without any additional charge. The Coast Guard is there for life-threatening rescue situations. However, they may assist boaters in distress by contacting a private rescue service and asking them to communicate with the vessel in distress. Fees for services by private companies are usually based on a set minimum, travel and return time, distances traveled, and other factors. The bottom line is they will not be cheap! It is worth your time to investigate signing up with a local marine rescue service, keeping in mind that paying an annual premium will be considerably less expensive than breaking down and finding yourself in a pay-for-service situation. If you trailer your vessel and boat on various waters, you should be sure to investigate a rescue service that has coverage in all the waters you expect to boat on.

Watercraft preparation: Before you leave the dock or launch ramp you should go through a basic checklist: fuel, oil, first aid equipment, operating radio and/or cellphone, anchor, dock lines, GPS, compass, credit card, and drinking water. It is wise to have onboard a quart of outboard oil as well, just in case. If any occupants are taking medication, be sure they have any critical medication along with them. If boating on unfamiliar waters a navigation chart would be very useful in pinpointing your vessel location should you need assistance. The Boy Scout motto of "Being Prepared" has never been more important than when operating a boat. Jet skis, also known as Personal Water Craft (PWCs) have special needs because of their limited size and creature comforts. A lack of shelter from the sun, rain, and wind can lead to hypothermia and or dehydration, which is always a concern on the water on any vessel. As in "The Rhyme of the Ancient Mariner" by Samuel Taylor Coleridge... "Water, water everywhere, yet not a drop to drink."

Float Plan: Be sure to let someone ashore know where you are likely to be going and a reasonable time to expect that you will be back. Being stuck on the water with no one knowing where you are, or even that you are overdue and "missing" is not a situation that you want to be in. A dead battery or non-functioning cellphone may prohibit you from initiating contact for help, so someone ashore who knows your boating plans could be your only means of initiating contact for help.

Episode 7

Captain's Log: *Sharks Bite*

Captain Robert Behling

Captain's thought for the day: Every day can be the beginning of the best day of your life. Enjoy the moment.

Background. I live in southern Alabama, and I like to occasionally fish far offshore. When I do, I find it is best to rely on someone who is on the water every day, and who knows the what and where of the local fishing. Over the years I have found a favorite charter captain I use for my offshore trips. Utilizing a good charter captain makes life much easier and generally your fishing is more successful when you are fishing waters you do not know well, or when you want to be fishing in a larger vessel that adds to your safety. Captain Earl charters a 29-foot Sea Hunt center console with twin 250 four stroke Yamahas. The watercraft has lots of speed and ample fishing room. It does come up a little short on creature comforts, but for a dedicated fisherman, that can be tolerated if it means more time for your line to be in the water.

Captain Earl was born in a hospital overlooking Biloxi Bay, Mississippi, and has lived around the water all his life. We call him a "Good ole Boy" because he is friendly, patient, and keeps us smiling with his stories of fishing adventures and growing up on the bay. He also does not like to wear shoes! I have fished with him in January, and to my surprise he did have on sneakers, but generally shows up wearing flip flops, which he takes off immediately upon getting in the boat. He will occasionally step on something on the deck that will cause him some pain and irritation, but he sees that as a small price to pay for giving his feet some freedom and keeping them cool.

To hear Captain Earl tell it, he has always preferred going barefoot. There was a time, before he started his charter business, that he worked construction. Jobs were often an hour or more away, and he hat-

36

ed to wear safety boots while driving to work, so he would grab his boots, throw them in the car, and drive off barefoot. When he arrived at the job site, he would put on his safety boots and begin working. One dark morning he was a little rushed, grabbed his boots without turning on the closet light, and hightailed it down the road. Upon arrival at the job site he found that he had brought two left boots from the closet! He had a choice, give up a day's pay and go home, or tough it out. He put the boots on; they obviously caused him some discomfort on one foot. His fellow workers told him he walked like a duck! The foreman kept calling him to the construction office to ask trivial questions, perhaps to give the other workers a chance to see him duck walk, or just to have some fun with him.

   Log Entry. Moving forward, I booked a fishing trip, and saw that Captain Earl was hobbling a little. "What's wrong?" I asked.

   He looked a little sheepish and began his tale of woe. He was offshore with a party that wanted to fish for shark, and they wanted to get

fish with some weight and size. The fishermen had two large black tip sharks on simultaneously, and Captain Earl brought the first one into the boat, removed the hook, and moved on to assist with the landing of the second shark.

In his haste to get into position to land the fish, he inadvertently came close to the first shark on the deck, which lunged and bit down on the front of his foot.

   When a shark bites down they tend to swing their head from side to side in a sawing motion, something Captain Earl wanted to avoid. One of the fishermen grabbed the gaff and tried to pry the shark's mouth open, but to no avail. Another fisherman grabbed a second gaff, and with one on the top and one on the bottom of the shark's mouth, they were able to raise the jaws enough to get Captain Earl's foot out. It was a bloody mess and they wrapped it as best they could, then headed for the dock. Once the boat was secured Earl was taken to the hospital emergency room, and the damage was serious enough they admitted him to the hospital and called for a specialist to take over his care. Reconstructive surgery and six days in the hospital, along with extensive physical therapy, repaired the wound and got the foot working again.

Epilogue. A year later I was fishing with Captain Earl far offshore for large red snapper when one of the fishermen hooked a seven-foot lemon shark. While Earl was cutting bait and helping others, the mate brought the shark onboard, flapping and banging the deck. Earl turned around when he heard the commotion and went ballistic. I should note that he was barefoot at the time!

"Get that **##** shark off the boat!" he shouted. This was the first time since I started fishing with Captain Earl that I ever saw him lose his cool. I know his mate will remember it for a long time. The mate managed to get the shark out of the boat through the transom door and get Captain Earl out of harm's way! The remainder of the trip focused on finding and catching red snapper, and when we had a shark hookup, we enjoyed the fight until those very sharp teeth bit through the leader.

Future offshore fishing trips with Captain Earl usually included a message that no sharks will be brought on the boat without first clearing it with the captain! We know the excitement of landing a large and powerful fish, and the urge to put it on the deck for pictures. Just be sure that everyone on the vessel knows what is going on and is prepared to be safe around the flopping fish. Events can happen very quickly, especially on a vessel that is rocking with the swells. We all learned a lesson from Captain Earl's experience that fateful day.

I have also often fished for sharp nosed sand sharks while living on Cape Cod. These sharks run about ten pounds and about a yard long, and they do not have typical sharp shark teeth, the mouth is more like rough sandpaper. However, they are a fish you want to be careful of when handling as they tend to thrash around on the deck and are enormously powerful. They will knock over buckets, dislodge gear, and generally create a ruckus. My tendency was to grab for them to gain control until I caught the wrong end of a head swing and found my hand caught up on the hook that was still in the shark's mouth. After that I changed my handling technique, usually sticking the shark's head in a large bucket and cutting off the tail to bleed the fish before I try to remove the hook. This technique also contributes to a tastier flesh when grilled with a little zesty Italian salad dressing for a marinade.

Captain's Safety Tip: When fishing, it is wise to have some form of footwear on. Flip flops do not count as footwear, as they provide very little protection from foot injury. Stray gear on the deck can cause painful injury, and of course the presence of any predator fish—shark, barracuda, even bluefish—on the deck can present a significant hazard to your feet and toes. It is important to note that hands can also be exposed to danger when removing hooks or moving fish. I have fished for bluefish for years, and they are aptly named "snapper blues." When brought out of the water they will snap their mouths for several minutes. Even a small fish can give you the opportunity to let out a loud yell and bleed on your boat. Handle all fish carefully and be aware that they all can bite! We also need to be mindful of the bacteria that may be in the water or even in the fish's mouth can lead to infection if not properly disinfected immediately after the injury.

Episode 8

Captain's Log: *Watch Your Back*

Captain Robert Behling and Captain Hal Records

Background. In Episode 7 you were introduced to charter captain Earl, a lifelong fisherman living on Biloxi Bay. You read about the shark bite on Earl's foot, and the damage that was done. In this episode Captain Bob and Captain Hal each tell stories of hard impact pain and risk on the water. The first story takes place in the Gulf of Mexico and the second on Cape Cod.

#1. Back Pain in the Gulf. On another trip with Captain Earl, we encountered a completely different kind of emergency. I lived for many years on Cape Cod, fishing for striped bass and bluefish from shore in the surf, and from my boat. I have also fished the coastal waters from Cape Cod to Florida, the Gulf of Mexico, and offshore Hawaii, Washington, Oregon, Alaska, and Australia. I have seen a lot over the years, including mechanical breakdowns, electronic breakdowns, very dangerous weather changes and sea buildup, and unrecognized hazards.

Situation. My family enjoys fishing, and on occasion several of my children are visiting me at the same time. When that happens, I always try and book a charter fishing trip offshore. They enjoy the opportunity to tie into large fish, catch a variety of species that are great on the grill, and have some quality family time and experiences. I booked an offshore trip with Captain Earl, and brought my son, daughter, and son-in-law with me. We were going hunting for "Bull Reds," big redfish that test your skills. Our target was a series of barrier islands about 15 miles offshore that hold bait and attract some large redfish.

Log Entry. We boarded Captain Earl's 29-foot Sea Hunt (You remember Captain Earl) on a beautiful morning with little wind and sun-

40

ny skies. Before leaving the bay, we fished around some structure to collect additional live bait. We had live shrimp, the bait of choice for most of the local species, but Captain Earl has learned over the years that you never know what will work on any given day. A live well full of small croakers provides an additional bait option. The ride to the islands was smooth, and once we got there, we noted that there were some larger swells coming off the Gulf. We anchored up and tried various baits and fishing techniques, had a couple of short strikes that did not hook up. It was a slow morning.

Captain Earl decided to move into some shallow water where he had had some luck previously. As we were coming up to a sandbar the water quickly went from 15 feet deep to about two or three feet deep. Just as Captain Earl was about to shut down the power and position the boat a rogue wave came in (it was about three to four feet in height) and lifted the bow. When the wave moved under the boat the bow dropped hard, slamming down with a lot of force.

Unfortunately, my daughter was sitting on a bench in the bow that was not padded, just formed fiberglass. As the bow slammed down, she took the brunt of the force on her lower back. "What the heck happened?" she said. "That really hurt."

She was in obvious pain, so we laid her down on the bench to see if that would help. It didn't, and Captain Earl wisely decided that we needed to head for the dock. The 15-mile ride back was slow and a little bumpy, increasing her pain and suffering. We got her off the boat and into the car for the ride home with some difficulty. Once home she took some pain medication and thought it would take care of itself.

A week later the pain was still there, so she decided to consult a doctor to see if they could determine what was going on. She was worried that there was some muscle damage, or a heavy sprain that might need immobilization or some other procedure to allow it to heal. Mostly she was determined to find a way to reduce the constant pain. What the doctor found after a physical examination and x-rays was a surprise. She had three fractured vertebrae in her lower back. The fractures were such that she needed surgical intervention to correct the damage and stabilize her spine. The surgery would also relieve the pain once it healed. Shortly after the examination she underwent a two-hour operation, and the surgeon successfully repaired the damage to the vertebrae. I was surprised with what the doctor did: he positioned imaging equipment over the damaged area where the fractures were, and, using the screen image, he carefully inserted and positioned a needle into a fracture. Once he was satisfied that he had the needle in precisely the correct spot he put bone glue through the needle into the fracture. After four unique needle insertions he was able to glue and repair all of the damaged bone fragments. With extensive physical therapy after the surgery she was able to return to her normal functionality and is now pain free.

Captain's Safety Tip. You may remember from the "Foreword" section of this little book we made the following statement: "When underway we each assume the mantle of command by which regardless of our level of formal or informal preparation, we become singularly responsible for the safety and wellbeing of our vessel and all who sail aboard her."

This episode, "Watch Your Back," tells a tale of severe and painful results from an entirely unsuspecting and unforeseen source, a rogue wave in shallow water. Can we prevent rogue waves such as that shown here? Can we foresee other potential dangers? Perhaps not, but we can react, not just the captains but also crew and passengers, for our own personal safety and wellbeing. Seating with thick cushions, spring or hydraulic seat suspension, and perhaps most effective and available of all, your legs, can help to prevent injury when a boat encounters precipitous drops due to wave and/or other boat wake situations. Does your boat have grab rails and grab handles in appropriate positions above and below decks, fore and aft? If grab devices are available, it is easier for people to hold on with their hands and bend their knees. From this position it is possible to rise to a standing position, thereby using one's leg muscles to soften or at least partially absorb the impact of a boat hitting water hard. Hitting with legs straight and locked can break bones as seen in this episode.

#2. Protect Your Back. As a case in point Captain Hal was returning to Narragansett Bay with friends after a frustrating day of tuna fishing in Cape Cod Bay. Frustrating because we could see schools of 100-plus pound tunas all day long, but they were not feeding and would have absolutely nothing to do with live, dead, or plastic baits that were chummed, trolled, or drop lined. Anyway… that is a story for another day. This is about getting beat up by hard impacts with water. We were on my friend Don's 31-foot Cabo sportfish boat with a pair of large Cummins diesel engines. She was rigged with a tuna tower and a pair of 12-foot outriggers, a very substantial and seaworthy vessel indeed. After giving up on the playful, but not hungry tuna, we moved back into the Cape Cod Canal and headed south into 20 knot winds that were pushing seas northward the length of Buzzards Bay up into the canal and our path. At the time the tide was running strong to the south and out into Buzzards Bay.

The opposing mass movements of water coming from the north and high winds coming from the south when combined with shoaling water depths at the southern entrance to Cape Cod Canal created huge waves that looked like walls of water. Having been there before I knew full well what to expect. We were going to take a beating as soon as we rounded the last bend of the canal. We scrambled to secure the outriggers and expensive fishing gear and take our positions in the pilot house, which was well equipped with grab handles everywhere they might be needed.

As we slowed to about 12 knots of speed it felt like we had just fallen off a cliff. Seas in the canal channel were suddenly 10 footers and the boat proceeded to climb and then fall precipitously and then crash into each successive wave. It looked as if we were all doing an exercise regimen as we kneeled and then stood at each drop, always holding on with at least one hand and arm. We could not slow down to reduce impact and still maintain steerage in the seaway. This continued for about half an hour until we cleared the channel and got well into the bay, after which we added power and ultimately arrived safely home in the wee hours of the morning.

Tragically about two years later, on the night of a severe thunderstorm, a rescue boat foundered in almost the exact same location at the southern end of the Cape Cod Canal while on its return to home port after safely getting a distressed vessel back to its home port. The sunken rescue boat was found the next day. Its captain, a young father, perished in the incident. Remember, even the most experienced captain may encounter weather or sea conditions that are dangerous and being aggressive in this situation often results in a bad outcome. As we saw in Episode 3, "Trouble at Fogland Point," knowing when not to go can be a lifesaving decision.

Episode 9

Captain's Log: *Off-Duty Rescue*

Captain Hal Records

In this episode, "Off Duty Rescue," things are a bit more relaxed as we experience something very unusual for a rescue boat captain: a couple of days off during boating season.

It was late August and my wife Janie and I were spending the last official weekend of summer on our faithful O'Day 27 sloop at our home mooring in Wickford Harbor. Janie is my lifetime and sailing soul mate. We have owned many boats, raised all four of our kids to love the water, and as she says we have more boats than brains. As you will see later on in Episode 11, "Keep the Open Side Up," Janie is a seasoned mariner and not afraid of the challenges of open ocean waters.

Wickford is a classic, quiet, historic New England village with marinas and lots of slips in the inner harbor, and a nice anchorage with great views of the bay from the outer harbor, which is protected by a stone breakwater. Outside the breakwater is a largely unprotected anchorage with a few scattered moorings. That very same breakwater provided great protection when the wind was up from the south as I was growing up in the 1950s. Now, whether you believe that global warming is impacting sea levels or not, it is a simple fact that normal, non-moon and non-storm tides are at least three feet higher than in those earlier years. Hence the breakwater is underwater on a normal high tide, completely invisible to mariners and providing much less shelter to the anchorage. So far no one other than boaters using the harbor pays much attention to this phenomenon. Someday, we hope sooner rather than later, the Army Corps of Engineers will wake up and raise the height of breakwaters all over this great land of ours to return to the level of harbor protection first achieved when the breakwater was constructed.

Rescue Boat

Log entry: The harbor was largely vacant as most boaters were combining this week with the Labor Day holiday to cruise to the islands and other ports. As with nearly every morning on the water I roll out of my berth, take out the crib boards, stick my head out the companionway and breathe in the fresh salt air, listen for the telltale sound of gulls, and the fisherman in me quickly scans the water for any sign of swirling water that might indicate menhaden schools and feeding bluefish or stripers. Fixing a quick cup of morning coffee starts the day off right. That was next on my list of things to do.

This morning my eye caught just a glimpse of something moving near the breakwater entrance, about 150 yards distant. Whatever it was moved slowly into the harbor, evidently struggling against the outbound tide. Perhaps it was a sleek cormorant just doing a surface dive to find fish below the surface, but it did not disappear below the surface. Maybe it was a small pod of menhaden or even a lonely bluefish on the prowl. But it did not look right. Maybe it was a shark since they do frequent the bay in late summer, but there was no pointed fin.

If it were late fall or early spring it could be a seal, but not at this time of year. Whatever it was, it had my undivided attention, even before our ritual morning coffee in the cockpit.

The harbor was very still at this early hour and our 11-foot Zodiac, *Dowser*, with its 25hp Merc lay tethered and still just astern. The mystery object continued to move very slowly in ever widening circles, probably some sea animal looking for breakfast, yet it just did not look right. That was it, enough mystery! Still perplexed I hollered down to see if Janie wanted to go with me on *Dowser* to see exactly what was going on. She popped out of the companionway ready for an early morning adventure, and we climbed aboard the RIB and off we went. The closer we got, the more it looked like a harbor seal, but again, not at this time of year. As we approached, a good deal of splashing erupted around the large dark black object in the water.

Oh my God, it's somebody's dog out here all alone and struggling to survive! We quickly pulled alongside the exhausted animal. It had a large black collar and did not resist as we pulled it in against the side of the boat.

Epilogue. The dog was a young black lab. He was quite large and must have weighed close to 100 pounds. Ever try to haul a big soaking wet animal over the sides of a RIB? The two of us struggled with this and we were eventually able to get him in the boat. The poor dog was trembling, exhausted, and unable to stand when we finally got him on board. I immediately felt guilty for not getting to him sooner. He appeared completely exhausted, and I do not think he would have survived in the water much longer. We took him back to our boat, got a towel, dried him off, and gave him water. We knew he was going to be ok when he stood up in the crowded cockpit of our sailboat, shook water all over us, tried to give us both a big smoochy kiss, and devoured the two hot dogs Janie gave him.

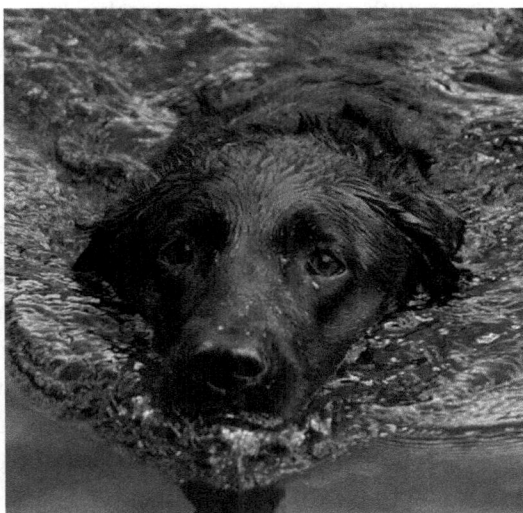

The sun was now up with its reflection flashing on the still calm water of the harbor. As we watched the dog regain strength our first thought was: to whom did this dog belong? There was no dog tag or identification on his collar. Did he swim out from the beach chasing a stick or maybe a seagull? Or did he jump or fall off a boat anchored outside the breakwater or perhaps moored safely inside? Janie and I decided the logical course of action was for us to cruise around the harbor in *Dowser* with the dog on board to see if anyone recognized him.

No Good Deed Goes Unpunished. After cruising around both the inner harbor and anchorage area inside the breakwater, no one recognized our four-footed guest. As a last resort and not really expecting success, we took a swing outside the breakwater. As we passed by an anchored 40-foot sailboat just outside, someone hailed, "Hey you guys in the dinghy with the dog!" at which point we motored over to the boat.

There were four young men aboard and one, evidently the owner of the dog, was irate. "Why are you stealing my dog?!" he yelled.

Without coming too closely alongside I asked if this was in fact his dog, and what was the dog doing swimming alone in the middle of the harbor channel against the flow of the tide?

He answered, "Yes of course the dog we had on board is my dog."

His answer to the question, "Why was the dog swimming against the tide in the harbor channel?" elicited a calmer response.

"Where was he swimming?" he asked.

I responded, "I was getting ready to have my morning coffee on our sailboat when I saw him swimming and struggling in the middle of the harbor channel. If we had been five minutes later in getting to him, you would no longer have a dog. He was totally exhausted when we finally got him aboard our dinghy." The dog owner finally recognized that we had not taken his dog; in fact we had rescued the dog from near certain death by drowning.

With the dog returned to his big sailboat and owner, we learned the dog's name was Winston, and that he was a one-year-old Black Lab. We collectively speculated on how he got off the boat, into the water, and ultimately into the harbor channel. The owner theorized that Winston jumped overboard sometime before dawn to swim ashore to do his business as dogs need to do. He had been trained early on not to do his business on the boat. Most likely he had been in the water for at least two or three hours, which would mean he was carried into the harbor and literally over the submerged breakwater on the inbound tide. He was then unable to continue making headway when the tide turned and began to run outward, uncovering the breakwater and blocking his way back to the boat, which was when we found him.

Captain's Note on Dogs Afloat. Many of us boat with dogs, and many dogs love boats and the water as much as we do. For many years we sailed with a springer spaniel who was very well behaved (generally better than our kids). This dog Tracey especially liked the dinghy ride ashore for her ritual walks, so much so that she would invariably jump out of the dinghy into the water and swim the last 50 yards or so beside me as I rowed ashore.

Many years later, our daughter brought along her 100-pound Weimaraner "puppy" whenever we went boating. That dog Elke loved to leap out of moving boats (sail and power) to try to catch passing seagulls and diving cormorants. Her legacy was, "There she goes again!" Even though she was a great swimmer, since she would unpredictably jump overboard we bought her a size large dog lifejacket and buckled her into it as soon as she got aboard. These things really work as do such items as doggie boarding ladders.

We are told that not all dogs are good swimmers, so if you are planning to add a canine to your crew, you may want to research which breeds are most likely to adapt readily to the vagaries of life aboard ship. If you already have a dog, or your guests bring a dog, do not be afraid to insist that they bring along a correct fitting lifejacket. Remember, the captain is responsible for the safety and wellbeing of his <u>entire</u> crew.

Episode 10

Captain's Log: *Fire on the Road and Other Boat Trailer Nightmares*

Captain Robert Behling and Captain Hal Records

In this episode, "Fire on the Road and Other Boat Trailer Nightmares," Captain Bob and Captain Hal briefly leave the water and tell stories about boats and trailers on land. The first is "Fire on the Road," the second is "Designer Sunglasses," the third is "Broken Axel," and the fourth is "Breakdown on the Interstate."

I woke up to a beautiful New England fall morning; the view out my open window was clear skies and warm breezes. I was living on Cape Cod at the time, and enjoyed getting out early and fishing, clamming, and just enjoying time on the water. I trailer my boat, and the launch beach with an improved ramp was an easy five-minute drive from my home. When I woke up this morning, I was hungry for a bowl of New England clam chowder. I knew the perfect spot to harvest some chowder clams. I checked my fuel supply and threw a clam rake and basket in my boat, hooked up the trailer to my truck, and headed for the ramp. I could almost taste the chowder that I would have for lunch. I was looking forward to a successful clamming outing.

#1 Fire on the Road. Sometimes, things just do not work out as planned! As I headed down the narrow country road towards the boat ramp, I thought I smelled a hint of smoke. I checked my rearview mirror and, sure enough, there was smoke coming out of the trailer wheel well. I quickly pulled off to the side of the road the best I could, as there was no breakdown lane, and jumped out of the pickup to investigate. I had a serious problem. My tubular trailer axle had rusted out, and near the spindle on the driver's side the axle shaft had collapsed and bent, bringing the tire in contact with the fender support, causing friction, and ultimate-

ly the fire and smoke. I had installed bearing buddies to keep constant lubrication on the spindle so it would turn freely even after constantly being submerged during launch and retrieval in saltwater, but I had no way to protect the axle itself from the ravages of the ocean water.

The immediate danger of fire was over, but now I faced the problem of what to do next. I was pulled off to the side of a two-lane road with a bent axle and nowhere to turn around to return home. The tire was not burning, but it was still rubbing on the fender support, and was being held there from the weight of the boat on the trailer. Fortunately, the tire did not burst so the boat was still upright.

I was not far from the landing, so I decided to slowly make my way down the road to the ramp. There should be less friction and heat buildup driving slowly, and I thought I could make it to the beach without a serious problem. I did, and managed to back down the ramp, release the boat tie downs, and launch. It was not pretty, but the boat was safely in the water. With the weight off the trailer the pressure on the axle causing the tire to rub on the strut was reduced, and while it did not roll smoothly, it did seem to be safe to tow the trailer back to my house. I secured my boat on a friend's mooring in the harbor after removing and loading my clamming gear and anything else that might be pilfered into my truck, as I did not have a lockable cuddy, and slowly headed home with my wounded trailer.

After a thorough inspection I determined that the axle was not repairable, so I visited a local shop and we found a solid axle with the proper dimensions to work with my spring shackles and trailer width. I removed the old axle, fitted the hubs to the new axle, and installed it on the trailer. I then went back to the launch ramp, loaded

my boat on the trailer, and brought it safely back to my home. I should note that there was no clam chowder for lunch that day, much to my dismay.

Rescue Boat

Safety Tip: Regularly inspect your equipment, especially when boating in saltwater. I don't think I would have spotted the rust eating through the tubular axle—water had infiltrated inside the tube and it was rusting from the inside out—but regular inspection will uncover many potential maintenance issues and safety hazards that can be corrected before they become a problem. It is also a good idea to inspect your trailer after you launch, as there may be issues that are hidden when your boat is secured on the trailer. I make it a habit to unplug the electrical connection from the tow vehicle just before launch and then plug it in again after hauling. This helps to prevent electrical shorts.

If you are having some rust issues with your boat trailer, you may also be having some rust issues with the vehicle that you use to launch and retrieve your boat. Because we have shallow ramps on Cape Cod, it was necessary to get the truck's rear axle and tires wet every time I launched and retrieved my boat. I inspected the trailer hitch mounting regularly for rust and deterioration, but never thought of checking the truck rear spring shackles.

One day the mounting bolts on a spring shackle rusted out and released the shackle, causing the entire rear end to shift backward, and the driveshaft came out of the spline! The truck came to a very abrupt stop. Fortunately, I have AAA; this was not something I could fix alongside the road. I had the truck towed to a shop and the repairs made. I am now much more careful with any equipment inspections that I make.

#2 Designer Sunglasses. Heading out for a day on the water stirs excitement, and a good friend and I had plans to take his boat offshore and look for bluefish and striped bass. My friend tends to use his equipment to the fullest, and his usual trade in for an upgrade involves a trip to the junkyard to dispose of the old worn out equipment. We secured his trailer (which was well used and prone to minor problems from time to time) to his truck and after a quick breakfast headed down the road. Just a few miles into the run to the launch ramp there were some strange noises coming from the trailer, and he said there was a pull to one side. He pulled over, got out, and crawled under the trailer looking for the cause. It was a sunny morning and he was wearing his designer sunglasses on our drive to the launch ramp, and they inhibited his ability to see

what was going on under the trailer, so he took them off and laid them aside. He immediately saw a loose axel connection, called to me to get him a wrench, and he tightened it up and felt the problem was solved. Anxious to get on the water he quickly crawled out from under the trailer, hopped into the truck cab, and we were on our way. *Crunch!* We both heard it and knew immediately what it was. No more designer sunglasses.

Safety Tip: The cardinal rule around boats is: Do not get in too much of a hurry; when you rush you often forget or overlook something important. In this case we were fortunate that there were no safety issues created by his haste, but he did do a lot of squinting trying to deal with the bright sun on the water. The good news is we found the fish and came home with a nice catch.

#3 Broken Axle. As described in this episode, boat trailering is not a trivial exercise and should not be taken for granted. There are only two kinds of people who use boat trailers: those who *have had* difficulty with trailering, and those who *will.* On a different occasion I had an axel literally break off on a roadway in the parking area of the launch ramp. I was towing a 20-foot inboard outboard boat at the time. In this case, I rented a boat trailer from a nearby Taylor Rental, unbolted and removed the winch and winch post from the broken trailer, lowered the tongue of trailer to the ground, then backed the second trailer over the tongue of the first trailer and proceeded to winch the boat directly from the broken trailer onto the rented trailer. Because my intent was to launch the boat for the season, I launched it with the rental trailer, then went back and winched the broken trailer itself onto the rental trailer and took it home.

#4 Breakdown on the Interstate. Larger rescue boat service providers often offer trailer coverage for a nominal extra charge. For example, I pay $179 per year for top-of-the-line watercraft towing coverage and an additional $14 per year for trailer coverage, hence a total cost of $193 per year. I also have AAA coverage on all my vehicles, so why would I spend the extra $14 per year? Case in point, I was towing an 18-foot center console from Rhode Island to Florida on Interstate Route 81 via Scranton, Pennsylvania. Although it is about 150 miles longer than

the Interstate 95 route south, it is invariably three to four hours shorter in time due to avoidance of the New York – Philadelphia D.C. traffic melee, hence a faster, safer, more enjoyable towing experience (if there can be an enjoyable towing experience). This route takes me from Scranton on Route I-81 to Route 77 south of Blacksburg, Virginia, and through the big hills of Fancy Gap into North Carolina and then Route 26 into South Carolina. It was here on a lonely stretch approaching Walterboro, South Carolina, late at night that I too smelled smoke and felt the single axel trailer pushing the truck left. I pulled to the side of the road and found the hub of the left wheel throwing grease all over the wheel well, and it was too hot to touch. Obviously, a blown bearing set.

My first reaction was to call AAA, but as a rescue boat captain who recommends the extra tow service to customers, especially at boat shows, I thought this a great opportunity to test what I was selling. I called the usual Rescue Boat 800 number for service. I expected at least a chuckle when the agent asked my lat/long and I told him Route 26 in South Carolina and about 150 miles from the nearest saltwater. I did not even get a chuckle out of him, and I knew I was ok when a man with a deep southern drawl came on the line and asked, "Now exactly where are y'all?"

Half an hour later a flatbed tow truck arrived, winched my whole boat and trailer onto his truck, told me I could pick my fixed trailer and boat up at a nearby truck stop in the morning any time after 10:00 am. I thanked him profusely and went on to the nearest hotel I could find.

The next morning, I went to the truck stop as directed, found the little boat and trailer sandwiched among four 18-wheeler semi-trucks in the repair shop. The duty mechanic presented me a bill for $100. This included no charge for the pick-up from the highway and replacement of both the trailer's left and right wheel bearing sets. He apologized for his decision to replace both sets of bearings and for the high price, but he told me the right-side bearings would not survive the trip to Florida. (No joke, oddly enough the left and right wheels and bearings had been dunked in saltwater an equal number of times). In any event I was pleased to pay $100 for work that normally costs closer to $150 **per side** for the bearings. Bottom line is that I saved $200 and got quick service. Since that adventure I am an absolute advocate for buying trailer towing from your rescue boat service provider.

Getting Started

Safety Tip. We cannot depart the discussion of boat trailering without making a pitch for dual axel trailers with brakes on both axels. In the above broken trailer scenarios, the situations would have been much less hazardous if Captain Bob and I were both using dual axel trailers. A single blown tire on a single axel trailer can cause the boat and trailer to whip, possibly spinning the tow vehicle out of control. It is less likely that two tires on one side will rupture simultaneously and hence towing can be continued safely, though be it at reduced speed. If your boat weighs anywhere around 2,500 pounds or more, a dual axel trailer could be a good investment, especially if you will be towing on high speed roads such as interstates.

Nowadays brakes are required on all axels in many states. Trailer and boat length and weight for this mandate varies, so you will need to check with the appropriate registries for the states in which you will be towing, not just the state in which your boat is registered. Remember the very same "Safety First" rule applies whether your boat is "on the hard" (land) on a trailer or at sea.

Part 2
Getting to Know Us

Episode 11

Captain's Log: *Keep the Open Side Up*

Captain Hal Records

In Episode 11 Captain Hal tells the story of a rough water rescue at sea and a subsequent dangerous journey home. "Keep the Open Side Up" is a kind of dark humor shared by rescue boat captains. The alternative is, of course, to roll or flip the rescue boat and sink, in which case we might not survive, let alone assist a vessel in distress.

Situation. It is again mid-August and I am assigned to our offshore rescue boat, cleverly known as Rescue Boat Three, a small but stout 23-foot Steiger with a pair 140hp Suzuki engines. Rescue boat companies frequently divide their assigned or covered geography into Areas Of Responsibility, affectionately known as an AOR. Within our AOR, the primary base and dispatch office are located at a marina in Narragansett Bay, and the satellite base is located at a marina in Point Judith Pond; not surprisingly the harbor opens directly into Block Island Sound and the ocean. We call this "out front" because it does indeed become offshore as soon the outer harbor called the Harbor of Refuge is cleared.

There is sort of a joke around the office where my nickname is Five-Knot Hank; this is because my preference is not to go to sea in winds over five knots. Strange things happen when the wind goes over five knots. Water gets rough, boats get hard to handle and dock, dock lines break, anchors pull, and the uninitiated, and sometimes even experienced captains, manage to do dumb things. The worst and most dangerous of these is when captains make the decision to go to sea when they should be staying in safe harbor, and to put a point on it, causing us to go out in those conditions risking life and limb to rescue them. Again, we have our little saying when we go to sea in unfavorable conditions, and that is the title of this episode: "Keep the Open Side Up."

Getting to Know Us

Mariners at Risk. Captain Bob relates a story about a friend we will call Lieutenant Toby, who was a Coast Guard officer during the 1960s stationed at Station Sault St. Marie, Michigan. This is a Great Lakes station, and the weather in this part of the country can get ugly, especially as winter approaches. One day while we were relaxing with a beverage, Toby told of his arrival at "The Sou." After orientation around the station and a review of the rescue equipment (remember, they had no cellphones, no GPS, and no satellite up-to-date weather reports), Toby said it was a bit overwhelming at first, but he quickly got into the routine. That is until they encountered some unbelievably bad weather, high seas, snow squalls, and lots of shifting winds. As he geared up to participate in a rescue operation, he noticed a sign on the wall of the ready room: "You have to go out: You don't have to come back." It was at that point that Toby began exploring career opportunities outside of the Coast Guard service!

Captain's Log: This day started quietly enough. No calls as of 14:00, I suspect because the wind was 15-20 from the southeast and predicted to increase. Small craft warnings would likely be posted soon. Even though I was on duty, my wife Janie had traveled down to our satellite marina and was comfortably installed at the pool. She did this because I frequently work seven days per week during the summer and it is the only way we get to spend time together.

So far so good, then at 14:30 my VHF radio crackled. "Dispatch to Rescue Three, Dispatch to Rescue Three."

I responded, "Roger Dispatch. Switch and answer 07." A new 36-foot Irwin sloop was in trouble about a mile west of the entrance to Block Island Channel, which is approximately 14 miles offshore.

Rescue Boat

What is the situation and what are the coordinates of the vessel? I hustled up to the pool to tell Janie I was off, but she asked to come along. The boss captain had given permission for her to join me whenever she liked because she is a certified lifeguard, an accomplished sailor, and loves boats. What a woman!

15:00 hours, 14 August. Janie and I cleared the breakwater nose-in to four-foot ground swells with a nasty little chop on top. We were able to maintain about 18 knots of speed so ETA on site was about 16:00 hours. As per usual protocol I telephoned the captain of the distressed vessel—let's call him Rob—as soon as we cleared the inner harbor.

"This is Captain Hank of Rescue Boat Three calling," and Rob replied he and his wife Jennifer were on a bare boat charter (no hired captain aboard) and had left eastern Connecticut via Long Island Sound at about 08:00. As the winds intensified, he shortened sail, then started their motor, and was in the process of taking the working jib down when its port sheet line somehow managed to whip through the snatch block and blow overboard. (Remember what I said about windy days?) You guessed it. The sheet line fouled in their propeller and stalled the engine, leaving them adrift with no operating sails and no operating engine.

I asked Rob for his current lat/long and if he was anchored. He said he was and that when he first called Rescue Boat the dispatcher suggested that he anchor if it was shallow enough for him to do that. Being in about 75 feet of water he did.

Rescue Boat Three is a 23-foot Steiger and has a pilot house and a small cabin in which are stored gasoline and electric dewatering pumps, tools, engine lubricants, lifejackets, and emergency gear such as pegs to drive into the hulls of boats that have been holed and are taking on water. Janie was wedged in the port corner of the pilot house facing aft in a heavy aluminum boat chair. Four to now five-foot seas are not comfortable at 18 knots in a 23-foot boat. Of course, we were both wearing our standard issue offshore inflatable life vests.

16:00 hours, 14 August. As Janie and I pulled near to Rob and Jennifer the wind had increased to about 25 knots and the seas to five feet. We could see that their anchor was holding and appeared to have adequate scope. Getting a bridle and hawser to them in this sea would be a tricky exercise. It was evident that we would need to toss them the hawser with a bridle attached and have them carry it forward and secure it, one end of the bridle to each of their forward cleats. The wind was now playing a gentle tune in their rigging and both boats were pitching up and down on the relentless seas. I moved in on their lee side and Janie was able to toss the lines. Rob caught them, secured the bridle, and was now firmly attached to Rescue Three.

"We are secured to the hawser and ready for a tow," Rob shouted over the howling wind.

16:30 hours, 14 August. With our towlines attached to their bow, I nursed Rescue Three into a position ahead of them and Janie payed out the hawser. We then took enough pressure on the hawser with our engines to slack their anchor line. Even at that Rob was unable to pull his anchor with his hands as Jennifer stayed at the wheel to keep their boat pointing into the wind.

I hollered out over the noise of the wind and sea, "Captain Rob, do you have an anchor windlass?"

He hollered back, "I don't know what that is."

I hollered back, "Step firmly on the large black button near your feet."

He accomplished this, all while he was holding the forestay for dear life as the boat pitched up and down, dunking him in salt water with each successive wave. As he stepped, the anchor started to come in and I kept enough forward motion on the two boats to relieve pressure on both Rob and the anchor, until the anchor was safely secured on its roller sprit.

17:00 hours, 14 August. With his anchor securely aboard Rob returned to the cockpit and took the wheel from Jennifer. On our return tow to the harbor he was able to keep the boat pretty much in the center of my wake. Once inside the harbor which was only a mile away, we shortened the hawser and put him alongside on the hip, then took him to a vacant mooring. He said he would have a diver come out in the morning to clear his propeller. Rob and Jennifer thanked us profusely. There was no charge for the service because the boat's owner had a commercial membership with Rescue Boat. I called dispatch on VHF Channel 16, "Rescue Boat Three, RTB" (Returning To Base, ready for reassignment) and got the anticipated response, "Roger Rescue Three, RTB."

17:30 hours, 14 August. Keep the Open Side Up. Given slowly but steadily increasing winds and seas, we wasted no time departing New Harbor on the west side of Block Island. We were able to maintain about 15 knots of speed with the wind and sea directly astern for about the first four miles while in the relative lee of Block Island, but thereafter we were barely able to hold 12 knots and the seas were six to seven feet. The wind was chopping off the tops of the waves and making them into blowing spray. It was beginning to be a challenge to keep the open side up. As little Rescue Three climbed the back of a wave, Janie's chair would skate down the now rain-soaked deck to the back of the boat, where she would brace it by putting both feet on the motor well. After watching her do this a few times, I thought that we might have the beginning of an idea for a carnival ride in a maritime theme park!

18:15 hours, 14 August. Water Moguls. We had two fundamental problems. First, I had to be really careful not to build speed going down the face of these waves because it would bury the bow of the boat in the incoming sea, and second, I had to add power at just right time in the trough of each wave to make it up the next sea and thereby keep the stern from get-

ting swamped. I watched ahead and Janie watched behind. She would tell me when to add power so I could keep my eyes glued to each up-coming wave and thereby prevent making us dive like a submarine.

As we approached the mainland, we hit the mogul fields. Those of you who ski know about moguls, steep little mounds and holes spaced close together that make a skier pay attention or maybe break a leg. Well, we have remarkably similar water moguls in heavy weather seas in areas where the ocean floor has steep hills and valleys, usually at depths of around 100 feet or so. A wave mogul is pictured above, and you can see the erratic behavior of the sea surface that could become extremely dangerous to a boater. In a mogul field, while trying not to become a diving submarine and not to get swamped over the stern, it is sometimes possible to steer around these peaks.

To make matters even more dicey, there was potentially dangerous weather around us that we were not aware of. Upon returning to the harbor we learned that tornado warnings had been posted while were in the middle of our crossing. Captain Keith in Dispatch discretely waited until we were safely back in the harbor before passing along that good news. Thank you, Captain Keith.

Challenging a rough sea in a small boat is great boat handling practice, but not recommended for the faint of heart. What was I saying about not wanting to go out in more than five knots of wind? Janie still reminds me of that rescue trip from time to time. A word of caution: If you think it is too rough to take a chance, do not press your luck. A delayed or missed dinner date is preferable to a lost boat and a very elaborate funeral. The open sea is a dangerous place to be when the weather kicks up, always exercise caution when making critical decisions.

Episode 12

Captain's Log: *Give Me Your Kids*

Captain Hal Records

Episode 12, "Give Me Your Kids" begins at the main rescue boat base near the head of Narragansett Bay. I was scheduled for the 07:00 shift, and as always cover both duty captain and sole dispatcher until either the 09:00 dispatcher/captain comes in, or I get called out on a run. My usual drill is to visit the local Dunkin' Donuts takeout window on the way to work for a sausage egg and cheese wrap and small hot regular coffee. In the rescue boat business, you never know when you will be able to get your next meal, so you eat when you can.

Each day upon arriving at the rescue boat base of operations, I check the log to see if there were any overnight runs and if any rescue boats are still underway. I switch the office telephone to my cellphone and walk down to the docks to check the boats. Rescue boats *Phoenix*, *Thor*, and *Alert* were all resting easily against their floating docks. You will remember that Rescue Three, the 23-foot Steiger, is berthed about 20 miles further down the coast. I board each boat in turn, first checking the main and auxiliary fuel tanks to be sure they are full, then check below decks for two and four stroke oil that is kept for customers should they need it. If any of the rescue boats are low on fuel and need topping off, Rescue Boat Service has a pickup truck with a tank of 100 gallons of gas that can be pumped via a long hose directly into the onboard fuel tanks. The rescue boats each carry anywhere from 100 to about 150 gallons of fuel in their main tanks, plus 10 gallons of gas and 10 gallons of diesel in portable tanks for customer needs.

Captain's Log: This was a special day. To begin with, the wind was only forecast to be five knots, my kind of day. It was late June and the local National Guard base was sponsoring an airshow with performances by the Navy's Blue Angels precision flight team at 10:00 a.m.

and 2:00 p.m. These were held at the old Quonset Naval Air Station on the bay and it is only about a 10-minute run from our docks to where the event is being held. These airshows draw spectator boats literally by the hundred. They come early and anchor near the end of the runway, usually much too close together. Given this event, Captain Keith, the boss, was due to cover dispatch at 09:00 and Captain Brian and I were to patrol the "observation fleet" and provide any assistance that might be needed. The Coast Guard and local harbormasters would keep a "no anchoring" safety area at the end of the runway just in case a plane needed to ditch.

08:45 hours, 24 June. Captain Keith arrived promptly at 08:45 and switched the inbound phone from my cell back to the office phone. He was in good spirits, not having had any overnight runs. I sat on the overstuffed sofa that served as a bunk for captains returning from late-night runs and sipped my now not very warm coffee. Suddenly the near-shore VHF lit up and the loudspeaker squawked out, "Mayday, Mayday, this is vessel *Poseidon*. I am a 20-foot Chapparal. I am rapidly taking on water and am sinking."

Keith responded, "*Poseidon*, this is Rescue Boat, what is your location?"

The response came back quickly, "I am in the bay near the fleet observing the airshow."

At this point I grabbed my go bag and headed for the docks. Keith would radio with more information when I was underway. When a call comes in stating the vessel is in danger of sinking, every minute counts. The quicker I can get on scene, the better the chance I have to save the passengers and save the boat. Humans always come first in any rescue operation, but if we think we can save the boat we will make every effort to accomplish this.

Rescue Boat

Captain's Note: Most rescue boat captains carry a "go bag." This bag can be a backpack or canvas bag and contains items essential for the captain to get through his or her shift. Mine contains water bottles, food, a small floating spotlight, a handheld compass, a jacket that can serve as a windbreaker and raincoat, whistle, first aid kit, a sheath knife, and as mentioned in Episode 5 "Don't Threaten Me," some captains carry a handgun. This is similar to what is known as a "ditch bag" that many boats carry in the unlikely event that their boat sinks. If you do not already have it, you may wish to add a ditch bag to your boat's gear.

09:00 hours, 24 June. Rescue Boat *Phoenix*, the ex-Coast Guard 26-foot aluminum RIB with a pair of 175 Suzukis was first in the queue. I boarded, started the engines, turned on the electronics and the strobe lights and headed out the channel as my radio came to life. "Rescue Boat *Phoenix* this is Dispatch; your target is on the north side of fleet not far from the entrance to our harbor. Four POB." (Persons On Board. Some captains refer to passengers as souls on board, but the acronym does not always sit well with people when transmitted over the radio.)

I added power before clearing the harbor (which we do only in the case of emergencies) and cleared the breakwater at over 30 knots. Almost immediately I could see the sinking boat. As I approached and slowed, I could see that the boat was going down by the stern. Two men were in the back of the boat with buckets and two young boys were in the front of the bow rider. No one was wearing lifejackets. Upon seeing me, the men stopped bailing. There were no other boats in their immediate area.

My first call to the men, let's call them Joe and John, was, "Don't stop bailing!" My second call to them was, "Give me your kids!" I quickly pulled two lifejackets that we keep for just such purposes from below, came alongside the boat, pulled the kids out of their boat and over the rubber tubes of *Phoenix* and told them to get the lifejackets on. I then threw two adult lifejackets into the sinking boat for the men, which they quickly put on as they continued bailing. No conversation was needed, they knew they were in serious trouble and very likely could end up in the water before this adventure was over.

09:15 hours, 24 June. With her engines idling in neutral I moved the rescue boat hand over hand from amidships of the sinking boat to her bow, and reached down over the side and clipped the large stainless steel snap on the end of the tow hawser to the bow eye of Joe's boat. I told the kids, ages about nine or ten, to sit down in the bow of Rescue One ahead of the forward tow post. That left the back deck clear for me to work the lines. I gradually payed out the hawser and simultaneously added power to get the boat in motion. I hollered to Joe and John to tell them what we were going to do, and to get ready. The boat was now half full of water, and we needed to move to action immediately. "Sit near the back of the boat and hold on. I am going to power up and try to bring you up to plane. If we can get enough speed it will cause the hull to stabilize and some of the water will spill out."

09:20 hours, 24 June. I could see a Coast Guard 34-footer headed toward me with blue lights flashing. The VHF sounded. "Rescue Boat *Phoenix*, this is Coast Guard 6194 on your starboard bow. What is your intent?"

I responded, "Coast Guard, my intent is to tow this sinking vessel into Allen Harbor at planing speed to keep it afloat, then beach it next to the town launch ramp."

The Coast Guard vessel responded, "Roger that, we will follow you as far as the breakwater." By now I was at planing speed, about 18 knots, with the tow 50 feet (two boat lengths) behind me.

Captain's Note: Under the right conditions, the bow of an open boat full of water when towed at speed from her bow ring will first point her bow upward toward the sky, and as she gains speed her back and transom will lift to the surface while quickly spilling hundreds of gallons of water over the stern, and hence, overboard. The boat will stay on top of the water for as long as she is being pulled fast enough to keep her on plane. Captain Keith in dispatch had been listening to the radio exchanges. He jumped in his truck and headed to the same beach where I was headed to provide whatever support might be needed.

Rescue Boat

09:25 hours, 24 June. I entered the fortunately uncrowded channel in this manner, being careful to avoid any underway vessels, rounded the bend into the main harbor and headed for the beach, vessel in tow, much as I had towed my little brother many times when we were kids water skiing, for a beach landing. Approaching the beach, I banked hard to port, let loose the hawser, and pulled back on the throttles. Joe and John got a Nantucket sleigh ride as their boat whipped forward like a slingshot and grounded not too gently onto the beach. Everyone was safe, and the boat did not sink, thereby saving the inboard/outboard engine from any damage from being submerged in salt water. Captain Keith released my hawser from their boat, and I hauled it back aboard *Phoenix*, then took the boys to a nearby floating dock, where they jumped off and were quite happy to be on dry land after almost finding out what it is like to abandon ship and get dunked in the ocean.

Epilogue. This entire rescue took about 25 minutes from time of call to the beaching of Joe and John's boat. The two boys, Tony and Ralph, seemed to be enjoying the adventure and were very well behaved. I thanked them both for doing exactly what they were asked to do exactly when they were asked to do it, which is safe and essential behavior in an emergency. I told them we were hiring at Rescue Boat if they wanted to be captains. The boys smiled and gave me back their borrowed lifejackets, and as they departed Rescue Boat *Phoenix*, the VHF radio sounded, "Rescue Boat *Phoenix*, Dispatch, two boats at the air show have fouled each other's anchors, four POB each boat, position lat …., long….,"
"Roger that Dispatch, Rescue *Phoenix* underway."
Later in the day when I returned to base, Captain Keith told me Joe and John's boat had blown the large O-Ring gasket known as bellows, by which the outdrive of its engine was attached to the boat, leaving a gaping six-inch hole below the waterline on the transom. This is a common problem with older inboard/outboard boats and motors. It is good they were close by, or the boat would surely have sunk before anyone could have gotten there.

Captain's Note: This rescue is a classic case in point about being prepared for an emergency on the water. Have adult, youth, child or infant lifejackets on board, and being worn in the case of children. Carry a readily accessible bailing bucket or in larger boats, have ready what we call a "bucket pump."

As shown here on the deck of Rescue Boat Three, this is a 1,000 to 2,000 gallon per hour 12-volt electric bilge pump with light gauge jumper cables securely wired to its red and black wires. The pump should have flexible and suitably long (four feet to eight feet) intake and discharge hoses and a six to eight-foot tether that can be used to raise and lower the pump into or out of a bilge. This whole arrangement fits nicely into a five-gallon Lowes or Home Depot type bucket, can be readily accessed, and can be moved anywhere on your boat or any other boat that you might be called upon to assist. The jumper cables can be quickly attached to one of your batteries. Such pumps may not be adequate alone, but they will, at the very least, help to retard the sinking process until help arrives.

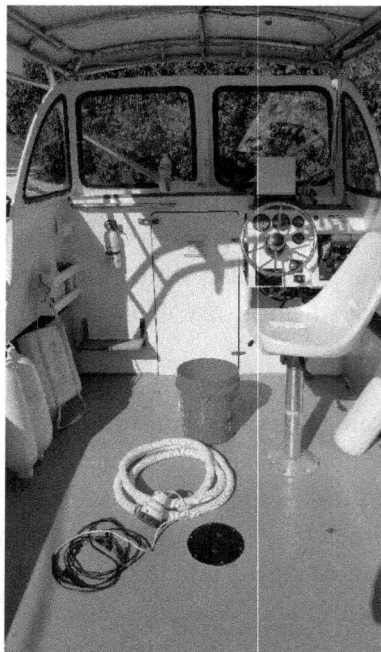

By comparison, rescue boats usually carry a 4,000 gallon per hour gasoline operated pump, and both a 2,000 gallon per hour and a 1,500 gallon per hour electric pump, giving them a dewatering potential from about 7,500 gallons to 10,000 gallons per hour depending on how the rescue boat is equipped.

Epilogue. In this rescue Joe and John had both a cellphone and VHF radio. A VHF has many advantages on the water. First, it reaches everyone already on the water in your area. Everyone, that is, who has their radio turned on to Channel 16, the emergency and hailing channel. Hence it is much more likely to reach someone who is near enough to help you. A cellphone, by contrast, reaches only one other party who is more likely not on the water, and may not even be available to answer

70

the phone. Remember, you may not have enough time to make a second call.

I cannot leave this safety discussion without asking each and every captain to do a huge favor for yourself and for those who will come to rescue you. **<u>Know where you are at all times.</u>** Be able to give your latitude and longitude on the first call for help. You can get this from a GPS or for free on a cellphone app. You wouldn't believe the number of distress calls we get and how long it sometimes takes us to locate vessels in distress. We will revisit this issue in subsequent episodes.

Episode 13

Captain's Log: *Hankering for a Cape Cod Fish Fry*

Captain Robert Behling

    Background. Living on Cape Cod makes meal selection easy: the bounty of the sea will provide clams, oysters, scallops, finfish, crab, and lobster, all you need to do is harvest what you feel like having. I had a hankering for a fish fry, so I started bugging my fisherman friend George to take me cod fishing. I did not mind taking my 17-foot De Quay Dory a mile or so offshore, but I was not about to go to the cod grounds, over 15 miles from the beach. My Del Quay was built in England using early Boston Whaler molds, and they laid down extra fiberglass, so it was unsinkable, very sturdy, and extremely seaworthy. I had a Johnson 88 pushing it, a bulletproof V4 that had been around for years. George fished a 25-foot Cape Codder with a 200 Mercury, designed for the near shore cod fishery and a very nice fishing platform.

    George called and said, "Ok, let's go cod fishing on Saturday next week." Unfortunately, I had a business obligation to be in New Hampshire that day that could not be changed. I had to decline, and thought I probably shot myself in the foot for any further cod fishing opportunities with George.

Rescue Boat

I first met George in the Cape Cod clam flats. I was getting lunch and he was digging clams for the market to pay the boat loan. He was an old-line New Englander, a retired high school teacher that surprisingly did not talk very much, a man of few words. He did take pity on me after we got acquainted and took me scalloping and taught me the ropes. I would occasionally bump into him while searching for clams, but when the weather was decent, he would usually go offshore for cod. He never said much beyond hello, but we soon became somewhat acquainted. One Friday he called and asked if I wanted to go cod fishing the next day. Unfortunately I had a commitment and had to decline.

Captain's Log. On Saturday I headed north to my appointment, and I forgot about missing out on the cod fishing trip, concentrating on the business at hand. Sunday, I decided to get some clams and make a chowder, so I headed down the road to my favorite clamming spot. When I got there George was sitting on the tailgate of his truck, a blank stare in his eyes and his hands were shaking. I thought he might be having a stroke or some other medical issue, I had never seen him like this before. I walked over and joined him on the tailgate, and we sat there for a few minutes. Finally, I asked, "George, are you having some kind of a medical problem that I can help with?"

He was quiet for a bit, then started his story. "I went out to the cod grounds yesterday and had a good catch. While fishing a strong wind came up, and upon returning home when I got to the cut in the Chatham bar the tide was rushing out, hit the wind, and created a tremendous turmoil with waves piled on top of each other. It looked a little like the inside of a washing machine on high speed."

George has been fishing all his life, and he knows the waters of Cape Cod as well as anyone I know. He usually does not take risks, but he had about 300 pounds of cod on board that he wanted to get to the market and get paid. "I looked at the cut and decided I could power through the rough water and get to the inner bay and my mooring." He said he lined up the boat, hit the throttle, and powered into the turmoil. The waves were very close together, the wind was blowing hard, and the tide was running out very rapidly. "My boat climbed up a wave, rode the crest and pulled the prop out of the water, so I had no control. A gust of wind hit me, turned the boat sideways, and I broached. There was nothing I could do to control the situation, and I went into the water. I was wearing slicker bibs, my slicker, and high rubber boots. I felt like I had an anchor on my legs, but I gave it all the power I had, popped up above the surface, saw my boat was overturned and reached out and was able to grab the leg of my outboard, which had stalled by that time. I managed to kick off my boots, climb up the transom of the boat, and get out of the water."

Chatham Coast Guard Station sits just behind the overlook for viewing the Chatham bar and the cut to the ocean. A tourist saw George clinging to his boat and called the Coast Guard, who immediately moved into action and sent a boat out to rescue him. He managed to hang on until the Coast Guard arrived on scene and returned to the beach cold and wet. He got a ride home, and spent the night reliving his experience. He was still in a state of shock the next day when I encountered him. Upon hearing his story, my first thought was *I could have been on that boat!* I will always be thankful that I was not.

Epilogue. A few days later George caught a ride out to his camp on the Chatham bar, and low and behold, his boat had washed up on the beach in front of the camp. It was a total mess; the hull was severely damaged, and the motor had been in the salt for so long it was ruined, so there was nothing to salvage. All his fishing gear was gone, as well as safety equipment, charts, fuel containers, etc. There was truly nothing left of value. We always wondered how the hull knew where to wash up so George would find it. This event happened many years ago, but I still reflect upon it from time to time. If I had been on board could I have convinced George to wait for the wind to die down, the tide to subside, the passage to become safe? Would I have even tried? I will never know. I do know that I never got my fish fry that week!

Captain's Note #1. A more recent incident found me aboard a charter making an offshore run to fish for red snapper. Captain Earl, who was introduced in earlier episodes, fishes out of Biloxi Bay in Mississippi, and is one of my favorite charter captains. On this morning late in June, Captain Earl had me fishing with two out-of-state guests. The two

Rescue Boat

guests had limited fishing experience but made up for it with maximum enthusiasm. The weather was unsettled, and Captain Earl was concerned. He told us we would wait and see what developed on his weather map before heading out. Because we would be going far offshore, he wanted to be careful and avoid problems. Finally, after half an hour, Earl spoke up: "I think the weather is going to go around us, and we have a window of opportunity to get out on the water. Let's load the live bait and get moving." You may remember Earl has a 29-foot Sea Hunt with two 250hp Yamaha four stroke engines.

A very seaworthy craft, with adequate power if needed to avoid getting caught in a dangerous situation.

We headed out and got about 15 miles offshore before the weather shifted, and Earl got nervous. He told us he wanted to shut down and watch the progress of the storm. In the meantime, we would fish while anchored. Almost immediately one of the fishermen hooked up and

was in for the fight of his life. After a good tussle he landed a large jack crevalle, probably over 20 pounds. This was the biggest fish he had ever caught, and was he excited! Earl got more and more nervous as he watched the progress of the storm, so I looked at the radar weather map and saw there were not one but two storms, one coming from Texas and the other coming from Florida. We were anchored at the point where it looked like they would converge! They were extremely fast moving, and before we knew it, they collided above the boat with thunder, lightning, heavy rain and lots of swirling wind. Earl went into high gear to retrieve the anchor, secure all the fishing equipment, and get the heck out of there. "Everyone get down in a low spot and hang on. I am going to make a fast run for the dock." Just as he spoke the storm intensified and shook up all of us. Bobbing around under a thunderstorm is not on my list of things I like to do.

Captain Earl pointed the boat towards the bay and firewalled both throttles. The rain was so heavy he could not see out the windscreen, so he stuck his head out around it and looked like a guy on a carnival ride. A little scared, windblown, wet, and wanting to be someplace else. I don't know how fast we were going, but I have never gone that fast in his boat before. Ten minutes later we outran the thunderstorm and just had rain to contend with. When we finally docked the boat, we were all soaked to the skin, a little shaken by the experience, but happy to be safely ashore. Earl apologized for the wet ride, but I could see that he would do it again if he had to. No fish fry on this trip either!

Captain's Note #2. When we travel a long way to experience the excitement of an offshore fishing trip, we hesitate to give in to weather and stay home. There are times, however, when the smart move is to exercise caution and not put your life or watercraft at risk. This would be especially true if a thunderstorm is imminent and you are fishing in an aluminum boat. Every year I hear of someone fishing quiet water in a metal boat that gets a lightning strike, often killing the fisherman. The smart move is to get off the water and live to fish another day.

Episode 14
Captain's Log: *Dunk Your Brother and Other Stories*
Captain Robert Behling

When Captain Hal and I start thinking and talking about our experiences, there are always a few that seem to pop right up. In my case, they usually involve getting wet! In this episode Captain Bob tells four stories. The first is "Dunk Your Brother," the second, "Danger at the Mouth of the Columbia River," the third, "Good Samaritan," and the fourth "Incident at America's Cup Races." As I think about them, there comes to mind a basic lesson we should all learn. When your attention is diverted, things can happen very quickly. Safety on and around the water should always be number one.

My first story goes back to my youth. I grew up with two brothers, and we were always out on the water, in the woods, or doing both on a camping trip to an island on a local river. There were no video games or TV shows beyond *Howdy Doody* and *Ed Sullivan*. Daylight was time to be outside, preferably digging worms, heading to the fishing spot, or borrowing a canoe and exploring the river.

#1 Dunk Your Brother. When I was about ten years old my mother informed us that her aunt, who lived on Long Island Sound and had a 30-foot Chris Craft, invited us up for a weekend cruise. Wow, a cruise on a big boat was nirvana for a ten-year-old boy who had never been in anything larger than a 12-foot wooden rowboat. My brothers and I were all looking forward to a very exciting weekend. The Chris Craft was on a mooring in front of their home dock because of shallow water, so we needed to dingy out from the dock. It took a couple of trips, and we were excited to get the adventure started. Instead of tying the dingy to the mooring, Uncle Ed tied it to a stern cleat and towed it about 15 feet behind the cruiser. It did not take us long to figure out that riding in the wake in the dingy was a lot more fun than sitting in a chair with the "old folks" talking about family memories. So, my older brother leaned on the transom, grabbed the dingy line, and pulled it in to the stern. He handed me the rope, told me to hang on, and he climbed down to get into the dingy. He was 13 and had convinced us he knew everything about everything, so he got to go first. Unfortunately, as I leaned over the transom to hold the rope, I caught a lungful of stinky exhaust, coughed, and the reflex caused me to let go of the line. Just as I let go my brother stepped down to get into the dingy, which unfortunately was now about five feet behind the cruiser. *Splash!* He went under, missed the prop, and I saw an arm come up just as the dingy passed him by. He grabbed hold of the gunnel, and I shouted to Uncle Ed that my brother had gone overboard.

The looks I got were scared, frantic, and mad. Fortunately, the cruiser came to rest, my brother climbed into the dingy, and we pulled him back and he got on board. Unfortunately, that was the end of our riding the wake. I never did get a chance to try it. Obviously, my brother never got a chance either, but he did create a memory of what it was like to be the "man overboard" while on open ocean water. We never thought of the dangers involved when we dreamed up these stunts, we thought it would be fun so let's do it. When on the water, it is often difficult to separate the fun from danger.

#2 Danger at the Mouth of the Columbia River. My next story puts me in a situation that I was totally unprepared for. I was just married and living in Oregon at the time. I was invited to join a party on a 32-foot Owens cruiser to fish for king salmon off the mouth of the Columbia River. Wow, what an opportunity for a young guy who loves to fish.

The marina was in Ilwaco, Washington and we loaded our gear and headed into the Pacific Ocean. The captain told me, "The salmon congregate at the mouth of the river waiting for just the right time to go up and spawn. They are in their prime right now and are wonderful eating." I had never fished for salmon, so I hesitated to jump in and get a line in the water. I was sure there was some rigging that had to be done, and I was right. They used a planer to get the lines down; this was before the use of downriggers and cannonballs. We set out our lines and trolled

Rescue Boat

around about a mile beyond the Columbia Bar. The sun was shining, and I was nodding off with the warmth and the motion of the boat. Suddenly the captain shouted, "Fish on. Bob, you take it." I didn't need to be told twice.

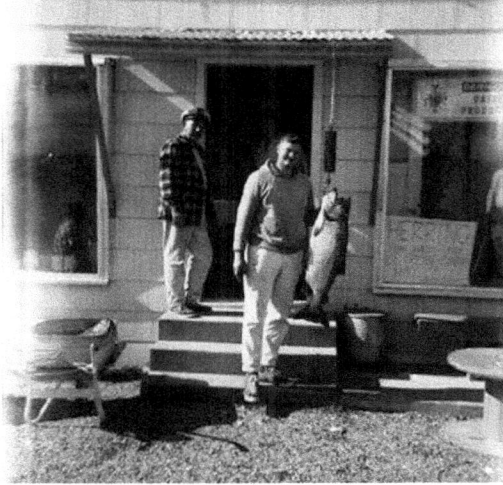

The captain advised me to, "Take it easy, don't horse him in or he will break off. It looks to be a nice one." After about 20 minutes I got my first glimpse, and it surely was a nice one. I was able to bring him alongside the boat, the captain netted him, and I had on the deck a nice 30-pound king salmon. Wow! That was the only fish for the day, and as the sun started to drop in the sky we headed back to the marina. As we came up to the bar my heart jumped into my throat! Going out there were two to three-foot waves, not much current running, and it was an easy ride in a 32-footer. Now the waves were six to eight feet, crashing and all jumbled up as they crashed over the bar, and even the captain seemed a little concerned.

He told me, "The Coast Guard has a special rescue boat they use here because of the dangerous turbulence over the bar at certain times. They strap the crew down and the boat can turn turtle, go completely over, and right itself." Oh My, what have I gotten myself into this time! Time to put the lifejackets on, hang on, and trust the captain. I also secured the lid on the fish box—by golly I was not going to let that fish get away if we got in trouble.

Captain's Note. More than 60 years later, I still feel that I never want to go through something like that ever again. It was probably the first time I ever put my complete trust for my life in the hands of a stranger. Fortunately, the captain was very good, and while he got us all wet, he managed to keep the boat open side up. We got ashore, I got a picture of my fish, and gave thanks for a safe journey. That was the last time I ever fished the mouth of the Columbia. I have fished many times off the mid coast of Oregon, caught silver salmon, sea bass, large floun-der, assorted bottom fish and ling cod, but never caught another king salmon until I took a fishing trip to Alaska in 2015. For that one, the waves were about one foot and there was no wind. I liked it much better.

#3 Good Samaritan. My first experiences with Cape Cod were as a boy on summer vacation in the 1940s. There were no interstates at the time, travel was slow, and the Cape was magical and still very pris-tine. I fell in love with everything about the place, and over the years I spent many wonderful vacations on the Cape, finally moving there to live for about ten years. I always had a boat, always fished for both fin and shellfish, and struggled as the neighborhoods changed, trophy houses were built where fishermen used to live, and the primary bumper sticker read, "Chatham, a drinking village with a fishing problem." That told me it was time to move on and live somewhere else.

While living on the Cape I was out in my boat every weekend, and some weekdays as well. One bright and clear Saturday I encountered a 20-foot center console with three people on board hard aground on a sandbar. They hollered out to me, "Can you help us get off this sandbar? We don't want to wait for the tide to rise."

I told them I would try, but their boat was bigger than mine, and I might not have enough go power to move them. "I'll come up to you, toss a line, and you can hook it on your bow cleat. I will try a side pull to swivel you off the bar and pull you out to open water." I was concerned with the depth, but with my Del Quay Dory I only drew about 10 inches of water; they probably drew over two feet.

I got close, tossed a line, and they secured it to the bow cleat. I secured it to my stern cleat, calculated my angles for a swivel side pull, and one passenger decided to lean over the rail and watch the line as I put tension on it. As I took up the strain on the line I applied power, and when their hull broke loose from the suction of the sandbar the line snapped tight, came up and hit the passenger in the head, and knocked off his glasses. They went overboard among the propwash and swirling sands, forever lost. I was able to get them off the bar, but I am sure their outing was ruined with the lost glasses.

Rescue Boat

Captain's Note. Many of us who spend time on the water have learned that it is wise to have a neck strap on your prescription glasses or sunglasses; you never know when they might come loose. I also have a clip on my hat that I can secure to my shirt, I have lost a hat or two while underway and when a wind gust blew it off. The lesson here is to try and think about what might happen and plan your activities to keep bad things from happening. Mariners will generally help strangers in trouble on the water; we know that there may be a time that we are in need. I had never pulled a watercraft off a sandbar before, and it did not occur to me that when the line became taut and the boat broke free the line would snap upward. A simple, "Stand back from the line while I add power," would have prevented this incident.

#4 Incident During America's Cup Races. For several years I was part of a sailboat racing team on Narragansett Bay. A friend owned a 32-foot Beneteau ocean racer, and he knew I was a motor guy with limited sailboat skills. One day my friend Rob asked, "Bob, would you like to be on our sailboat racing team for the summer races?"

I looked at him and said, "Rob, why in the world do you want me on the boat? I don't know very much about sailing, especially on a large boat like yours."

His response was somewhat comical. "I don't need you to have sailing skills; I will take care of that. I need you for strength and ballast! Wind the winches on the sails, move around to even the weight distribution on deck, things like that." Not a great esteem builder! I should say that at a hefty six foot two I was bigger than anyone else on the team. The story begins in Narragansett Bay, Rhode Island.

The bay was crowded with boats heading out to see the final race of the America's Cup, which would take place offshore about 12-15

miles offshore. Rob got the team together and we brought spouses and made a day of it. When we arrived at the race location there were lots of large, leased party boats with props churning the water to keep position for the best sighting, and the ocean was a bit of a mess.

After a couple of hours of milling around, the race was called; not enough wind for racing. Everyone headed for the dock, the big party boats in the lead. As we were coming in there was an 18-foot O'Day sailboat putting along under power from a five-horse antique outboard. Just as we came up to the small craft the captain was pulled backward against the transom; his outboard bracket had come off and the motor was flipping around and not attached to the boat. It finally got dunked and shut down, and he pulled it inside the cockpit.

Captain Rob hollered over to him, "Can we help you; do you need a tow to shore?"

He hollered back, "Thanks; that would be great. My motor is dead." We were under power not sail, so we idled up and threw him a line. I noticed that his cockpit deck was covered with empty beer cans, and his passenger was looking a little wobbly.

He secured the line, and Rob hollered over, "Where do you dock your boat?"

He hollered back, "I brought it down from Boston on a trailer and launched at the boat ramp."

Rob hollered back, "Ok, which ramp, and we will tow you there."

Silence. It turns out there are probably a dozen ramps in the vicinity of the races, and he had no idea which ramp he launched from, and therefore left his vehicle and trailer in the parking area. "I don't know, you know, THE RAMP." He had no idea where his trailer was.

Captain Rob hollered over, "I will tow you to the marina, and you can see if they will help you locate where you left your trailer. Good luck." We got him to the dock, retrieved our towline, and motored to our mooring at the marina.

Epilogue. I don't know what happened to the little blue sailboat with the inebriated captain, I am sure he eventually found someone to take pity on him and help him find his trailer. I don't think he should have been driving, especially towing a boat, but I will never know if he

Rescue Boat

made it home safely. It looks like, as you will see in Episode 16, Captain Hal's request for captains to, "Always know exactly where you are," is almost as important on land as it is at sea.

Episode 15

Captain's Log: *On Becoming a Boat Captain*

Captain Hal Records

In Episode 15, "On Becoming a Boat Captain," Captain Hal looks back at the how and why of achieving his goal of qualifying as a rescue boat captain, with an eye toward helping those who might wish to explore the opportunities and understand the challenges and rewards found when serving as a rescue boat captain.

When asked what his job was like, a lifelong friend and retired US Navy pilot once told me that landing an F-14 Tomcat fighter on the rolling deck of an aircraft carrier is the most fun a person could ever have with clothes on. Well, being a rescue boat captain also has its moments. You can go from complete boredom spending an entire day in dispatch waiting for a call that never comes, to back-to-back hair-raising rescue adventures that most people only read about.

You do not do this job for the pay, which although reasonable, is generally not commensurate with the everyday risks to life, limb, and property that rescue boat captains take on a regular basis.

Captain's Log. August 2005. How it all started. I have been on the water since my father, a US Merchant Marine officer in World War II, took me on boats before I could walk. I served in the US Navy in the late 1960s and have owned too many sail and power boats over the years to count. My wife Janie says, and correctly so, that we have always had more boats than brains. Hence when I first contemplated becoming a rescue boat captain, I thought I had a pretty good handle on what the job might entail, but little did I know.

Other than paying my annual membership fees for years to a local rescue boat company, I never paid a lot of attention to what they do. That all changed when our daughter Sarah started working for one of these companies as dispatcher while she was in high school. She started telling strange, unusual, and funny stories about her workday while at the breakfast table every morning. By the end of the summer I could not wait to get to breakfast to hear her latest story. She kept saying, "Dad, you should come over and meet Captain Keith, you will like him." And so, I did.

Captain Keith was owner of a national rescue boat franchise and he invited me for a ride along the next weekend with one of his captains, which I did. That experience piqued my interest and I asked Captain Keith if he had any openings for rescue boat captains, and what would be the qualifications. He said, and I quote, "I always need good captains. There never seem to be enough to cover our 7 day a week, 24 hour a day, 365 days per year operation." He said that if I wanted to apply for a position, I first needed to get a US Coast Guard "Six-pack" license, which permits a captain to carry up to six passengers for compensation. Most fishing charter boat captains hold this license. I also needed to secure a federal TWIC (Transportation Worker Identification Credential).

Captain's Log. Getting your license and TWIC. This was in August. That very week I signed up to take the captain's course given by a local certified instructor. There were about ten would-be captains in the group, and we met two hours per night once per week for eight weeks. The instructor was Coast Guard certified and was excellent. We worked hard doing readings, homework, and navigation exercises, and I passed the final exam at the end. That qualified me for the license of Operator of Uninspected Passenger Vessels (OUPV) and to carry up to six passengers, hence the title Six-pack. It should be noted that both Captain

Bob and I know people who have lots of experience on the water who have not been successful in passing this course. The examination is no-nonsense and extremely challenging. I also took the optional two-week extension course to complete modules for sail-auxiliary and commercial towing endorsements on that license.

If you are interested in knowing more about getting your captain's license, and would like detailed information on what is required and how to go about it, go to the US Coast Guard's National Maritime Center website at http://www.uscg.mil/nmc. It has complete listings of everything needed for captain licenses and the federal TWIC (Transportation Worker Identification Credential). Most people who apply for these licenses have already completed a basic boating safety course, are in reasonably fit physical condition, love being on the water, already know basic seamanship, and truly enjoy helping people who are in real need of being rescued. It also helps to be a bit of an adrenaline junkie, such as a lady captain who worked with us for a number of years and who has previously sailed around the world in a 30-foot sailboat single-handed—talk about courage!

Captain's Log. May 2006. Season 1. The next summer I reported to work at Rescue Boat armed with my shiny new license, and just a little bit of extra ego. My agreement with Captain Keith was to work for free for the first week, then decide if I wanted to continue, and more importantly, if he wanted me to continue. During that first week I completed ride-along runs with different captains and got to handle the different rescue boats. It was my first time handling and maneuvering twin engines, and I also learned to use their electronics: Furuno Radar and GPS. I found all this a bit challenging to digest, but also very interesting.

On the last day of my trial period upon return from a run, Captain Keith was on the dock and beckoned me into Rescue Boat *Phoenix*, the 26-foot RIB described in Episode 5, "Pending Weather." He was going to have me take him out so he could personally evaluate my boat handling abilities before putting me on the payroll, or not. No problem.

I stepped over the tube, into the cockpit of the boat and into the pilot house ……oops! As I put my go bag under the console and looked up, I could see that every one of the forward and side facing windows were completely covered with cardboard. Visibility forward and to the sides was zero. Captain Keith calmly said this was to be a simulated fog exercise known cleverly as the "cardboard fog" and that I was to take the boat off the dock and out of the busy channel and perform the exercises he requested using instruments only. He would stay on board to alert me if we were about to crash into something. Seriously!?!

I fired up the engines, lit up the electronics, cast off the dock lines and got underway, moving ever so slowly but surely out of the slip, around the docks, and into the long narrow channel while watching boats moving around me on the radar and channel markers on the radar and GPS. At the end of the channel Captain Keith said to increase engine RPMS to 4,000 and proceed north to Buoy 6, which I did while very carefully watching the instruments and realizing that 4,000 RPMS on *Phoenix* was about 30 knots, 36 miles per hour, which as you may know is quite fast on the water. Captain Keith then said, "Cut close to the buoy, then make a hard-starboard turn and head back to the channel." I did cut close to the buoy, maybe a little closer than he would have liked, and rounded back toward the channel after which he said, "Ok, slow down, put her back on the dock and try not to run over anybody." Really!?!

This I did, still blind due to the cardboard fog. Two duty captains, Mark and little six foot three Dan, were awaiting our arrival at the dock, each with grins looking like the cat who swallowed the canary, and they helped me to secure the lines. Isn't it interesting that they had not found it in their hearts to tell me what to expect for a final test of my boat handling? Captain Keith now had the same grin, shook my hand, and said welcome to Rescue Boat Captain Records, and then said for the first time I ever heard it, "Being a rescue boat captain is not for everyone." As mentioned in Episode 3, "Trouble at Fogland Point," I have heard this said many times since, usually at auspicious moments. I have also seen many new wannabe rescue boat captains come and go. Some lasted only a few days on the job, or until a particularly challenging rescue, and a few stayed on for many years.

Epilogue. And that is how it all started. The next winter I went back to "Boat School" for another four weeks and upgraded my license to master captain, which bumped me up to a 25-ton license. Upon each five-year license renewal and with appropriate sea service, the tonnage was upgraded to 100 tons. My captain's license as shown here is very similar in appearance to a passport.

After having had more than fifty years on the water when I started this adventure, I thought I knew a great deal about boating, the sea, and being on the water in all kinds of situations. Even at that, I am still in awe at what really goes on with boaters out there in the bays and oceans, and as it turns out I don't know enough, even after all these years captaining a rescue boat and over 1,200 rescue runs. I again remember the sage advice of my long-departed friend Bob Daigle: "I will teach you to sail in half an hour, and then you can spend the rest of your life getting good at it." Boating is fun, but the sea is an unforgiving master and safety must always be the first concern for captains and crews alike.

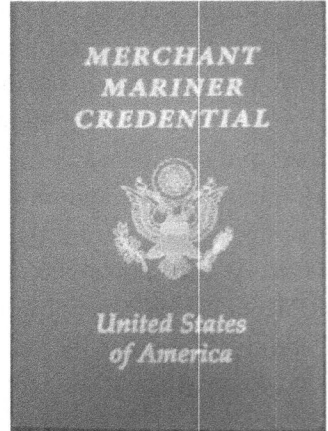

Episode 16

Captain's Log: *Where Are You?*

Captain Hal Records

In Episode 16, "Where Are You?" Captain Hal tells three stories about the importance of always knowing where you are: #1 "I Have Run Aground," #2 "My Engine Has Failed," and #3 "Mayday, Mayday." Brace yourself as this story ends tragically.

Place yourself and a couple of friends in your watercraft enjoying a day of boating. Suddenly a storm front moves in and there is a dense fog, preventing you from seeing any landmarks. You have not been paying a great deal of attention as you motored along and talked fishing. Suddenly your motor hits a submerged log, bends the prop, vibrates erratically and stops running. Do you know where you are right now?

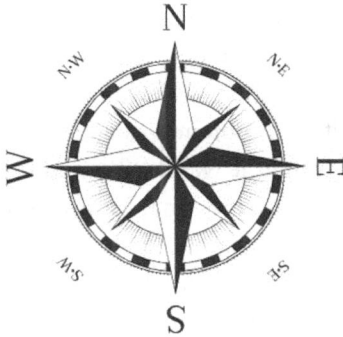

Do you know your latitude and longitude? Do you know how to get your location quickly? Who do you think cares about where you are? Do you care where you are? Only you can answer these questions. If Captain Bob and I seem obsessed with this issue, we are, and in this episode, through words and illustrations, I will hopefully make you as concerned about where you are at all times on the water as are those who must come to your rescue when you have an emergency that prevents you from returning to port on your own power.

When I first started working for Captain Keith at Rescue Boat I was amused when callers could not readily tell me how to find them. It was surreal, like Ogden Nash's little poem, "The little man who wasn't there, he wasn't there again today, oh how I wish he would go away." As it turns out the whole process of at sea rescue starts with one question: Where are you? The rescue process is quite simple in theory. Step one is to first get to the distressed vessel, step two is to hook them up to the rescue boat, step three is to tow them home or provide a jumpstart or other service, and step four is for the rescue boat to return to base, or move on to the next distress call as the case may be. This sounds simple enough and it is, if the caller can tell the rescue service exactly where he or she is. This episode tells the tale of three emergency situations, each escalating in severity, and each stumbling on the first step of the rescue process: Where are you?

#1 I Have Run Aground. It was a clear and breezy afternoon and I was assigned to the offshore boat, Rescue Three, at our ocean-side base. I got a cellphone call from Captain Mark at Dispatch. He told me that all three of the northern rescue boats were out on runs. He was very busy and sounded a bit frustrated, saying he had trouble getting details from a caller, and would I call him back to follow up on determining what his problem was and what needed to be done? Roger that. I checked my watch, it was 14:30, and then I dialed the cellphone number Captain Mark had given me. I noticed that it had an out of state area code, which was somewhat unusual.

What sounded to be a middle-aged man answered my phone call. Let's call him Lester Jester. He told me, "I am in a 24-foot center console boat with three friends. We launched at a boat ramp, but I don't know what town the ramp was in. I am stuck and firmly aground, and not in any danger. We are near a bridge; I can see it clearly from where we are." When I asked what bridge he was looking at, he didn't know. He said, "I am not from around here, and I am not familiar with the names of any of the bridges." Off the top of my head I can think of about a dozen bridges in our Area Of Operation (AOR).

I asked for Lester's latitude and longitude and I might as well have been speaking Greek. He had no idea. I asked what the bridge looked like and his description generally fit six of our bridges found as far as 50 miles from my rescue boat berth. It is now 15:30 hours, a full hour has elapsed and I have still not left the dock. I asked if he had a VHF radio, which he did, so I asked him to radio me on our working channel, 7. Although most VHF radios can be toggled for a transmission/reception distance of 2 or 25 miles, the further away the signal is generated the lower the signal and voice strength. This signal was strong even at the lower setting, so he was most likely in my end of the state. Perfect. It is now 15:45 and I am still at the dock. My next step was to leave the dock and head for the bridge closest to me. At 16:00 I found him perched on a sandbar just beyond the Great Island Bridge in Point Judith and almost in sight of the ramp where he had launched his boat. It took about 15 minutes to refloat Lester Jester, after which he and his friends continued motoring on their merry way, still somewhat uncertain of where they were and where they might be going.

This story is about a boater using a bridge for navigation. The other response we get too frequently is, "I am near the red Number 2 buoy." Do you have any idea how many red Number 2 buoys are in our AOR? I suggested to Lester that he might want to invest in and learn how to use a GPS/depth sounder, especially if he was going offshore where there are no bridges by which to navigate. I could see from his expression he probably thought the idea would be too much trouble, so he would likely continue to navigate by the seat of his pants!

#2 My Engine Has Failed. It was 22:00 hours on a dark foggy night in late July. I was working dispatch at the main base up in the bay and as with most July days it had been busy. I was tired and ready to go home when a cellphone call came in. The caller sounded rattled. Let's call him Fred. He was in a 28-foot Wellcraft Offshore Fisherman with four friends and had lost his engine and all electrical power. His cell signal was weak.

Ok, my first question is, "Where are you?"

Fred answered, "We left Point Judith two hours ago and steamed generally south and east travelling at about 15 knots."

I asked—you know what I asked—"What is your latitude/longitude?"

His response was, "My GPS isn't working so I am not sure."

My next question was, "Do you know how deep the water is where you were last fishing?" Water depth can sometimes help us to narrow down an area.

Fred replied that they had run another half hour nearly due south since they last fished. The depth then was about 100 feet. Translation: Fred had no idea how deep the water was at his current location, but for sure he was offshore.

At this point I used a second landline and reached the on-call night duty rescue boat captain, Wil, with a heads-up that he would likely have a run out front as soon as we figured out where his "target" was located. Even with the best "dead reckoning" navigation in the world it would be nearly impossible to find Fred. Even when we do have a latitude/longitude, if it is too deep to anchor, we need to estimate drift based on wind, tide, and sea conditions. It is very easy to miss the mark by miles over the period of an hour or two of searching. There was only one way to solve this mystery. I called the Coast Guard, gave them Fred's name, boat info, and cellphone number, and asked them to triangulate the cellphone signal before he ran out of power.

The Coast Guard responded quickly as always, and fortunately Fred had unknowingly made a giant circle in the fog and rain and was only about five miles southeast of the harbor from which he had departed. Captain Wil on Rescue Three was able to locate him and make contact, hook his towline to the disabled craft, and then tow him safely back to port. Had his cellphone died too soon, it would have taken a full-blown search and rescue mission to find Fred. It should be noted that commercial rescue boat services have a strong working relationship with the United States Coast Guard. As illustrated in this story, the Coast Guard has access to resources that commercial rescue services do not. The mission for both is very similar: assist boaters in distress, provide life-saving rescues, and when possible prevent a watercraft from going under. The rescue boat captain is responsible for helping the client, whereas the Coast Guard has many additional responsibilities, including protecting the environment from fuel leaks and spills, and to warn mariners of potentially dangerous debris in the water such as partially submerged pilings.

#3 *Mayday, Mayday.* This is a sad story, one that I was not personally involved in. It happened on a dark, clear, but moonless night in mid-July. At 01:00 hours a panicked female voice called over the radio

Rescue Boat

on Channel 16, "Mayday, Mayday, this is the power boat *Sponson*, we are in a wreck." A Mayday call, whenever it comes over the radio, sends chills up the spine of all mariners. Captain Keith, the boss, heard the very first call on the radio at his house. He immediately dressed and headed for Rescue Boat base about 20 minutes away. Upon arriving he could hear a good deal of emergency chatter on Channel 16 and Channel 22, the Coast Guard working channel. Rescue base has low side short range VHF and high side long range VHF antennas and receivers. In the 20 minutes it took Captain Keith to get to base, the Coast Guard, local harbormasters, fire departments, and various police departments from around the bay were executing their emergency plans to respond and provide required assistance and emergency aid if needed.

The person in distress, let's call her Lilly, stayed on the radio, responding to the emergency services requests for pertinent information. "I am just a passenger on the boat, and I know very little about boating and navigation," she responded to a Coast Guard inquiry. "I *don't have any idea where we are*, other than we left Portsmouth around midnight and had been underway for about an hour." Not good! Put a pin in the map at the harbor, stretch a string for an hour's motoring (let's say at about 20 mph), and you have a huge circle of water to cover in a search for the boat in distress.

It was now about 02:00 hours. The radio signal was reasonably strong, but the caller's voice was fading. There is a chain of large islands running north-south in Narragansett Bay, essentially dividing it into what we call the east and west passages. Warren Harbor, from which the vessel had departed, is about halfway up in the east passage, so the emergency response vessels were searching wide areas within the east passage. During the hour since the Mayday first went out, many emergency vessels had departed harbors in both the east and the west passage to assist in the search, with no success. It was now nearly 03:00 hours, two hours since the original call, and still no one could find the boat in distress. (Our rescue boat service tries to be on scene within 30 minutes of an initial call.) Lilly, the lady on the wrecked boat, could still talk and respond to radio communications. But it was obvious she was weakening, and for the present she was all the rescuers had to help them find the location of the wrecked boat. Lilly said that she was bleeding and the two men with her were badly hurt and one of them was not moving. Imagine her predicament: in the middle of the night, cold, wet, hurt, bleeding, and not knowing where she was and with both of her friends unable to speak. This is about as bad as it gets.

At about 03:15 hours the Coast Guard again asked Lilly, "What lights can you see?"

When asked that question before, Lilly had said she saw many lights, blue and red flashing lights. This time she responded, "I can see only one set of blue flashing lights. There are no other lights visible."

The quick-thinking Coast Guard radioman immediately called out on Channel 16, "Are there any emergency vessels with blue flashing lights that are alone and not near other rescue boats?"

The VHF response came quickly, "This is the Applewood harbormaster. I am running across the west passage headed for the east passage." That meant that the wreck had to be in the west passage, to the west of the islands, not to the east of the islands where the rescuers had been concentrating their efforts. This critical piece of information allowed responders to move the focus of their search to the west passage and hence on a much smaller area. The wreck was found on the rocks of tiny Gull Island in the west passage about 15 minutes later.

Epilogue. It was determined that the 21-foot inboard/outboard bowrider had run directly onto the rocks at an estimated 30 knots, immediately killing one passenger, critically injuring a second, and leaving Lilly with several broken bones and lacerations. The critically injured person later passed away in the hospital. Lilly had been thrown from the boat upon impact with the island, then crawled back into the wreckage to send the Mayday, which likely saved her life. When I reported to work on the morning after the accident, Cap-

tain Keith was still there, visibly shaken as he had listened to the entire thing on the radios, but was unable to do any more than was already being done by those on scene.

Subsequent inquiries determined that the accident was not a result of BUI (Boating Under the Influence), but rather of excessive speed and the now deceased boat's captain **not knowing precisely where he was**.

Episode 17

Captain's Log: *A Funny Thing Happened On The Way To*

Captain Robert Behling

It is not our intent to intimidate or scare you away from boating by focusing on the dark side of things and what can go wrong on the water. As you may have seen from the stories in Episode 16, "Where Are You," bad things do happen from time to time, but by using common sense and with proper preparation, boating can be enjoyed safely as a family and with friends.

Episode 17, "A Funny Thing Happened on the Way to…" is intended to lighten things up a bit and share some of the funnier things we have all experienced on and about boats and the water. It shares six little stories of a personal nature that are funny in retrospect, if not at the time they occurred. So here we go: A funny thing happened on the way to the…

#1 Heading for the Boat Ramp. When you hear the bite is on, the excitement builds, and you want to get on the water and wet a line right away. One Saturday a friend I fish with regularly called. "The flounder are in and biting, let's go get some." Flounder are one of my favorite table fare fish, and I seldom turn down the opportunity to target them. I told him I would meet him at his house, and we could trailer his boat about 12 miles to the hot spot. I must say we were anxious to get on the water, so our minds were racing ahead to baits, strategy, drift speed, etc. We hitched up and hit the road, excited and ready to do some serious fishing.

Rescue Boat

The drive to the launch ramp was through some hilly country, and after one uphill climb and hitting a bump at the top we heard this loud screeching!

"What the heck was that?" Tim called out.

"I don't know, but you better pull over so we can get out and take a look."

Fortunately, Tim had hooked up the safety chains because he forgot to secure the ball coupler latch and it came loose when we hit the bump, letting the trailer stem jump up and disengage from the vehicle. That small lapse in focus while hitching up his trailer could have cost Tim his boat. The fix was simple, we were able to reattach and secure the latch and head on to the launch ramp. Since then I always follow a checklist when I hook my boat to a vehicle, and I double check safety chains and the ball latch. Here is my checklist that you might find helpful:

Captain's Launch Checklist
- Adequate fuel/oil onboard
- Drain plug in and locked
- Bow tiedown secure
- Stern tiedown secure
- Trailer tires fully inflated
- Electrical connection for trailer lights tight
- Safety chains hooked up securely
- Trailer hitch secured to ball and latched

*#2 **Hand Catching Fish.*** Captain Earl, my favorite charter captain, tells this story of targeting cobia, one of his favorite offshore fish. I was not on this trip but heard all about it from Earl. On the way to the blue water he made a stop and had his party fishing around the Gulf of Mexico oil rigs, a favorite congregating place for all sorts of large fish looking for an easy meal. One of his anglers hooked up, and it was an exceptionally good fish, probably in the 40-pound category. After a good fight, the angler attempted to bring the fish onboard before Captain Earl had the net properly positioned, and as he lifted it over the side the cobia came loose! Captain Earl dropped the net and made a lunge for the fish,

got it in a bear hug, and was able to get it into the boat safely. During the tussle Earl managed to get struck in the chest with the dorsal fin but did not think too much about it. The fortunes of war as a charter captain helping an angler land a trophy fish!

A week later Earl found himself in the hospital with a raging infection in his chest. Those of us who live on the Gulf Coast understand that in the slack water, especially during the summer months when the water temperatures can get to as high as 90 degrees, there are all kinds of bacteria just waiting to attack us through a break in the skin. But Earl was many miles offshore, where did the bacteria come from? Speculation might look to the fish itself; perhaps the bacteria were living in the protective slime that most fish have covering their skin. Perhaps the bacteria had lodged in his shirt while he was getting sprayed launching the boat and was pushed into the wound when the dorsal fin stabbed him in the chest. Perhaps upon returning to the launch ramp, bay water splashed up and got his shirt wet, giving the bacteria a means to entering the wound. We will never know. All we do know is that that was an awfully expensive cobia! Not only did Captain Earl incur medical expenses, he was also out of commission as a charter captain for the better part of a month.

The moral of the story is: Do not ignore any wound when on the water, it can become a superhighway for bacteria to enter your body and create havoc. I am friendly with the local fire chief, and he told me his crew carries spray bottles of 50 percent bleach and 50 percent water to spray on any nick or cut they receive while on a rescue or any routine assignment. A quick spray is a good start, and if there is any penetration, a good cleaning when you get home will provide the ounce of prevention that we all hear about. You surely want to avoid the pound of cure!

#3 ...*Boat Ramp Again.* When you trailer a fishing boat, storage for your watercraft is often an issue. If you live in a climate where there is significant rainfall, when left uncovered the boat can fill with water during a storm, causing damage to your electrical system and stored items such as lifejackets, which are quick to mold when left wet. The solution is to remove the drain plug so the water can run out during a storm or purchase a boat cover. Many of us opt for removing the drain plug; it is much easier and quicker than installing a cover after every outing.

Rescue Boat

Most of you will know where this is leading. No, I did not forget to install the drain plug before launching my boat, what I did was forget to push the lockdown lever to tighten it securely in the stern drain hole. The launch activities created some water pressure on the transom, and lo and behold, as the boat entered the water the plug was pushed out. The drain hole is small, perhaps an inch or so in diameter, so the water did not come in quickly, and I did not notice it until I was underway and then stopped to fish. My feet got wet! Something was wrong, and I soon found what it was. I scurried around looking for the plug, finally found it, plugged the hole and tightened the lock down. A little bucket work and the bottom was somewhat dry again, and I was on my way, a little embarrassed that I could make such a simple mistake, but happy to have caught it before anything was damaged. If I had followed my own advice and carefully gone through the captain's launch check described earlier, the problem would have been avoided.

#4 Fishing Grounds. Years ago, I was on a deep-water charter out of Morehead City, North Carolina. Our objective was to fish the continental shelf, a two-and-a-half-hour steam from the dock. Upon arrival, the captain took about 15 minutes to position and anchor the boat, taking into consideration the tide, the wind, and the bottom structure. I spoke with him later, and he said the time spent is worth it. He told me the fish congregate over the structure, and if you miss it by even a few feet you will not have proper presentation of the bait. Getting the bait over the right spot will double the catch. I should have known this from my days fly fishing in Idaho, presentation was always critical to success when I was trout fishing. I have come to believe him; in my experience a charter captain that does not know how to, nor take the time to position the boat properly, will end up with dissatisfied customers (me included!).

The water we were fishing was about 120 feet deep, so it was a long drop and an even longer retrieve if you had a fish on. It was early in the season, and the boat was not overcrowded, so we all had lots of room. My wife was with me (she usually prefers shopping to fishing but wanted to see the deep ocean waters) and I started catching fish right away. She comes from a family of Wisconsin fishermen, but never caught the bug. She does like boating, though, and unlike my usual modest size fishing platform, we were on a 110-foot and very stable boat. They even had a food galley with a grill on board, so for her it was like a cruise ship for fishing

We were getting trigger fish, bee-liner snapper, African porgy and assorted modest size bottom fish. My wife was having trouble reacting to a strike and getting hooked up, and I began to heckle her a little. I know, I should have kept quiet, but I couldn't resist.

After a bit, the captain had heard enough, and he jumped down from his perch on the roof of the cabin and told her to reel up. Surprisingly she did this without argument. He grabbed her line as it came over the rail, pulled out a pair of clippers and clipped off both hooks on her rig. I just stood there and was speechless. The captain then reached into his pocket, took out a packet of Gamakatsu super sharp and expensive hooks, tied on two, baited the hooks and told her to let her line down.

When she hit bottom and reeled up three turns as directed, she immediately had a strike. She was a little slow to react but did manage a hookup, then stood there for a minute not sure what to do next. Another strike came, and I told her to reel up, which she did. After a few moments of cranking over the rail came a nice bee-liner snapper and an African porgy. If I could have captured the smile on her face it would still be priceless, for I had not had a double that day.

Now the heckling turned around, and I was the object of the snippy remarks. "What's wrong with you that you can only catch one fish at a time? It is much more efficient to get two on before you reel up, it saves energy and time!" I will only report the comments that were somewhat close to good taste, there were others that were more sharply pointed, reflecting on my obviously limited angling skills. I did notice the captain standing in the cabin deck had a smile on his face. During the rest of the trip neither of us caught another double, but I know for sure that it did not matter, she had her revenge. From then on, most times I went out on a charter I gave her the car keys and the credit card and told her to enjoy shopping!

#5 Fishing Grounds Again. My wife is an incredibly talented lady, but her idea of an ideal fishing trip is when I surf fish from the beach, and she can walk along and look for interesting shells. At times she might also agree to help carry some of my fishing gear if I decide to do some deep wading in the surf. I have come to understand this, but there are times I forget and invite her to join me on a blue water fishing trip. This happened when we were vacationing on the west coast of Mexico, and I decided I wanted to try for a sailfish. Perhaps in the back of my mind I wanted to catch one to get back at her for the double hookup years before when we fished the Continental Shelf. In any event, she decided to come along, not wanting to shop alone in the unfamiliar markets of Mexico.

The charter boat was diesel-powered and about 30 feet long, with a modest cabin and seating. We were trolling when I hooked up with a small tuna, which gave me a heck of a fight. The captain wanted to keep the fish for some ceviche, so he backed off on the power to get more control over the fish, and we landed it over the transom. He idled the boat to get the fish on board, and we had a following wind that blew the diesel exhaust straight into the cabin. The boat also got caught up with the waves and did some pretty good rocking. The combination of the two put my wife into extreme distress, and before I knew it, she managed to upchuck her breakfast all over my gear in the cabin. UGH! What a mess, and what a smell. I have never been seasick, but if there ever was a time, that would have been it.

She didn't speak much on the return trip, but if looks could talk, I knew it would be best not to ask her to join me on any more deep-water fishing trips. If she did not feel comfortable shopping, she could stay by the pool and catch some rays or sip on a margarita. I never did get a sailfish that day.

#6 Group Outing. My friend Rob, who captained the 32-foot Beneteau ocean racer sailboat, gathered the racing team together for a day sail and a picnic at the yacht club after our time on the water. Spouses were included, and of course they wanted to participate. Who doesn't like cruising Narragansett Bay on a beautiful sailboat with nothing to do but enjoy the scenery? And of course, the after party was attractive to our spouses as well.

We took off from the dock with a detailed chart of the bay and went sailing! Rob called out to his wife, "Jan, you can oversee map reading and navigation for this trip. Here is the chart of the bay, keep me advised if you see that we are getting close to any dangerous area, either low water or rocks. Remember, with a dagger keel the Beneteau draws over seven feet of water." Rob had recently upgraded from a 25-foot Catalina which drew much less water.

About an hour into the sail Rob hollered at Jan, "My instruments are showing that we are coming up on some shallow water. What does the chart say?"

Jan replied, "It looks ok, the chart shows over 20 feet all around us." A couple of minutes later we felt this violent lurch of the boat, and we came to an immediate standstill.

We quickly determined that we had run aground on a sandbar and dug the dagger keel in deeply. We reduced sail and Captain Rob asked to see the chart. Jan brought it to the wheel and as they looked at the chart she said, "Damn," and turned the chart upside down. She had been looking at the west side of the bay when we were sailing on the east side, she had the chart reversed! When correctly positioned, the chart showed between five and eight feet of water for the area where we had run aground.

Fortunately, Rob was experienced breaking away from having his keel stuck in the sand, and he put the main out to catch the wind and heel the boat over, had everyone aboard move to the "tipped down side" and then started the engine, positioned the rudder, and applied power. Amid much groaning the keel finally broke the suction of the sand and released, and we were able to back off the bar and continue our cruise. The moral of the story is that instruments don't lie, and when the depth sounder signals a warning of shallow water, regardless of what the chart says, that would be a good time for the captain to make the decision to head out for deeper water.

Rescue Boat

We regaled other club members with our "upside down chart" story during the after party. We had done well in the race the previous week, so this was a bit of self-flagellation that they all enjoyed. Captain Rob is a well-respected cardiologist, and seldom makes mistakes. While technically this grounding was not his sailing error—it was due to faulty map reading by his navigator—it still proved that we are all human, even Captain Rob. The racing team should have been on the alert and warned him, or at least confirmed what his instruments were telling him: Danger lies ahead. On this day we all fell a little short, but we recovered nicely and without any damage or injury.

Epilogue: There were no injuries to life, limb, or property, other than perhaps to my pride, in any of these six little "a funny thing happened on the way to..." stories. Nonetheless, each story makes a point that can save you from a similar fate.

Episode 18

Captain's Log: *I'm Sinking*

Captain Hal Records

Episode 18, "I'm Sinking," tells the tales of two on-the-water situations that had more serious implications to life and property. These incidents are grouped together because of a common theme: they both involve the imminent danger of a vessel sinking. The first story begins on a clear and breezy hot summer day. I was assigned to Rescue Boat *Phoenix*, the 26-foot aluminum hulled RIB.

Captain's Log 13:00 hours 23 July. Routine Milk Run. I was working the late shift and when I arrived at the dispatch office located at the head of the bay, I was sent out to move a 30-foot Monterey cabin cruiser whose engines had failed just outside the entrance to Warwick Cove Channel. The captain had been heading back to his slip in the cove.

Let's call him James. This was to be a classic milk run. It was daylight, clear weather, and I had James's lat/long position where he was safely anchored just a short distance from his berth. After securing a towline to the disabled boat and getting underway, towing James astern of the *Phoenix* on a short hawser, we proceeded into the long, winding, and busy channel. I called out on VHF Channel 16, "Securite, Securite Rescue Boat *Phoenix* entering Warwick Channel with a disabled power vessel on a short stern tow."

The VHF call "Securite, Securite," alerts channel traffic that we are present and have limited maneuverability. This is one of three levels of marine alert broadcasts for all vessels to hear on Channel 16. The most critical message, as you know, is "Mayday, Mayday," which means lives and/or vessels in imminent danger. The middle level alert is "Pan-Pan," which means a vessel is in urgent need of assistance. The more routine is "Securite, Securite." Securite is a lower level of alert which is informational and provides safety information to mariners. It is used by commercial vessels such as towboats and many ferryboats when entering crowded harbors.

We had just passed from the channel into the harbor when the VHF radio came alive on Channel 16, "Mayday, Mayday. I'm sinking." Rescue boats are equipped with two VHF radios. While towing we use a channel like 5 or 7 on one radio to maintain direct communication with the captain of the vessel we are towing. The second radio remains on the hailing channel, 16, so we can call out notices as in the Securite mentioned above, and also enables us to stay abreast of other things going on, in this case the Mayday.

When a vessel has only one VHF as do most pleasure vessels, it can be set to scan mode, which will scan other channels for inbound calls. Because of this James also heard the somewhat frantic Mayday call. A Coast Guard radio operator quickly responded to the Mayday, going through their standard list of questions to give them a better sense of what the emergency is and helping them decide how to respond.

Question 1 (you know this): "Where are you?"

The response was quick to come back. "Northeast of Rocky Point, latitude XXX, longitude XXX."

Question 2: "What is your situation?"

Response: "I am a 28-foot Bayliner cabin cruiser taking on water, my engine has stalled and will not restart, and the bilge pump cannot keep up with the seawater entering the hull."

Question 3: "How many people (POB) on board?"

Response: "Four people."

Question 4: "Is everyone wearing lifejackets?"

Response: "Yes."

The Coast Guard radio operator then said, "We are dispatching a boat from Castle Hill Station, ETA your position 45 minutes, 15:45 hours."

Captain's Note. When mariners are in distress the Coast Guard puts out an alert. The alert for this incident was: "Pan-Pan. This is Coast Guard Sector Southeast. At 15:00 hours a Mayday was received from a 28-foot Bayliner taking on water at location lat XXX, long XXX. Four POB. Any mariners in the area keep a sharp lookout for this vessel, report all sightings and lend assistance if possible. Coast Guard out." This message is repeated at periodic intervals until the vessel has been assisted.

Upon hearing the answer to where the vessel in distress was located, I knew it was only about two miles from my current location and about six minutes away at speed. I called James on Channel 7, asked, "Did you hear the Mayday?" He responded that he had. I asked him, "Can I temporarily secure your boat on a nearby dock so I can respond to the Mayday?"

James was cool, and an accomplished captain, and said, "Yes, of course." After moving James's boat to a nearby dock, I reversed direction and departed the channel at speed with the tow hawser in a pile on the deck at the stern of my boat. I was getting underway at about the same time the Coast Guard completed radio transmissions, and I was on scene within 15 minutes of the initial Mayday call.

Captain's Log 15:15 hours 23 July. Going Down. As always, when approaching a vessel in distress we look carefully at the situation and determine how to proceed. Human lives take absolute priority over boats and property. Losing a boat is one thing, but a boat can always be replaced. Losing a life is quite another. Once you are gone there is no coming back. Also, if we did something during the attempted rescue to lose the rescue boat and captain, there would be no one on scene to provide assistance or save anybody. For example, coming alongside a burning boat that could explode or tying up to a sinking boat that could drag down the rescue boat could be a fatal mistake. These rules should also be heeded by good Samaritans in similar circumstances.

The Bayliner was indeed taking water as the boat had settled such that her normal waterline was nearly a foot below the surface. This was definitely an emergency. The people on board were all senior citizens and the captain, let's call him Alan, was clearheaded, but obviously anxious and worried. Step one for me was to get the people off the sinking boat, then get some pumps set up and operating as quickly as possible. Rescue Boat *Phoenix* has limited deck space, with a pilot house, bollard tow posts forward and aft, and now the 75 feet of hawser piled up on the stern deck. There was not very much room to bring four people onboard and initiate immediate pumping operations to dewater the hull. Fortunately, there were four other good Samaritan boats varying in size from about 18 feet to 35 feet on scene; each boat had responded to the Mayday and subsequent Pan-Pan.

One of these boats, a 28-foot Cape Dory Trawler, was within easy hailing distance. The Cape Dory has relatively low sides, making the deck easily accessible for safe transfer of the passengers. Let's call that boat's captain, Joe. I asked Joe if he could approach on the starboard side of the sinking vessel and take the passengers onto his boat. He agreed and moved into position on the starboard side of the sinking boat. In the meantime, I would move my boat to the portside, get some pumps on board, and start the dewatering process.

Captain's Log 15:25 hours 23 July. We were in the process of doing this when Alan boldly announced that his passengers should move quickly to Joe's boat, but that he would not leave his boat. Seriously, Alan!?! Ok, this is no time to argue. I passed Alan a 2,000 gallon per hour electric pump, which he put into his bilge, and I connected it to *Phoenix's* starboard battery bank and immediately began pumping. By now Joe had taken Alan's passengers aboard the Cape Dory and had moved off to a safe distance. By the way, against general rules I had secured the *Phoenix* to the Bayliner with a single center cleat to cleat line with no half hitches so I could initiate a quick release if needed. Bear in mind that both boats are drifting side by side, beam to the wind, in a mild two-foot sea. I was dragging the heavy 4,000 gallon per hour gasoline operated water pump out of the pilot house when something to port caught my eye. During any rescue operation it is critical to maintain situation awareness and stay alert to whatever is going on nearby as well as on the boat in distress.

Captain's Log 15:35 hours 23 July. Captain Keith in Rescue Boat Three had heard the Mayday call and had also come to the scene to help. He lashed Rescue Boat Three, the 23-foot Steiger, center cleat to cleat to *Phoenix* and jumped across the two rescue boats and climbed into the Bayliner. He immediately went down into the bilge and could see and feel water flowing through a two-inch diameter crack in the engine's heat exchanger pipe that connected to a through hull fitting.

He yelled up to me, "Hank, get me some rags, a screwdriver, and a hammer." I found what he needed and tossed them to him. By now Captain Keith was knee deep in salt water in the bilge of the boat, and the water was within a foot of reaching the cockpit floor. He quickly drove the rags into the crack with the screwdriver and hammered them in as tightly as he could, significantly slowing the flow of water into the boat. The combined pumps were now dewatering the boat at a rate of about 6,000 gallons per hour and were barely keeping up with incoming water until the temporary rag plug was jammed into the crack. Once the water flow into the hull was substantially reduced, we could see and feel the boat rising, and soon were able to see the water level receding. All this time Captain Alan was watching patiently and helping wherever he could. A brave soul to be sure.

Epilogue. Captain Alan's Bayliner did not sink. Good Samaritan Joe delivered Alan's crew back to the dock from which they had departed earlier in the day. Captain Keith and Rescue Boat Three towed Alan's boat with Alan still aboard to a nearby marina travel lift where it was hauled immediately upon arrival. Rescue boat captains, or Rescue Boat Dispatch if the captain is too busy, will call ahead to make haul-out arrangements with the dock staff when an emergency occurs. Most marinas are extremely helpful in this regard, and frequently clear their lifts and have a crew standing by to assist with a quick haul-out. There is no better feeling than getting a sinking boat safely out of the water and onto the hard ground, commonly known as "the hard."

The Coast Guard had arrived on scene at 15:40 hours, but immediately departed on another call as soon as they learned that Alan and his crew were safe. The Coast Guard then broadcast on Channel 16 for all to hear, "Cancel Pan-Pan of 15:00 hours. Vessel has been assisted." (As you will see in later stories, "vessel has been assisted" can mean quite different things.)

Rescue Boat

Captain's Note. At 16:15 hours, about an hour after I originally left him, and as Captain Keith towed Alan to the marina for haul-out, I returned to Warwick Cove Channel and radioed the patient Captain James from where I had left him. Captain James had by now been towed to his dock by a friend. He asked if everyone on board from the Mayday call was ok, and I said, "Yes, thanks to your patience and understanding."

Over the years I have from time to time needed to leave an in-process tow to respond to an emergency. On one such occasion I left a boat full of fishermen at anchor in the Harbor of Refuge in Point Judith to rescue a couple with young children offshore. When possible, Dispatch will send another rescue boat to complete the tow, but true to Murphy's Law these things seem to happen on our busiest days when all rescue boats are on runs and frequently have a backlog of work. You would be amazed at how many people need assistance on the water on any given day.

Captain's Log. Another sinking. 21:45 hours, August 6. I was covering dispatch and was the only captain on duty at the time. Official-ly, our duty shifts have posted start times but not end times. This is be-cause we never know where we will be, or what we will be doing at the anticipated end of our shifts. It would not be very practical, or even pos-sible, to punch out at the end of an eight-hour shift and go home if we were 20 miles offshore looking for a distressed vessel. True to form, on this day just before quitting time the low side VHF radio sounded.

"Mayday, Mayday. This is *Iron Bottom.* I have hit the rocks and am sinking." He had to be within about 10 miles since the low side radio was loud and clear, so I grabbed a handheld radio and my go bag and headed for the docks. The handheld radio enables me to stay abreast of developments as I am walking and setting up the boat. This night *Falcon,* a 26-foot ProCat catamaran with a pair of 175 Suzuki outboard engines, was in the outboard slip so I boarded, set her up, and headed out of the nearly empty harbor with red and yellow strobe lights flashing.

21:55 hours, August 6. The Mayday caller, let's call him Tum-bleweed, sounded a little tipsy, but he did know where he was. When asked for a location, he responded, "I am on the northern tip of Prudence Island," which is about 12 miles from our Rescue Boat base. His boat,

Iron Bottom, was yet another Bayliner, a 26-footer. The Coast Guard radio operator responded to the Mayday and gathered from the distressed captain relevant information following the procedures described in the preceding story. Harbormasters from both sides of the bay also quickly responded to the distress call.

22:30 hours, August 6. It was pitch dark and I was the first to arrive on scene and began looking in the water for a sinking boat. I knew it was not sunk because Tumbleweed was still on the radio. I moved ever closer to the rocky beach at the tip of the island and scanned the area with *Falcon's* search light. Tumbleweed was panicking. He was still on the radio and said, "I cannot swim, but I am wearing my lifejacket, so I am going to jump overboard before the boat sinks. I will try to get to the shore."

I could see flashing blue and red lights in the distance so knew there would be additional help here soon. At that point I spotted the boat about 100 yards from my location and watched as Tumbleweed jumped off into knee deep water. *Iron Bottom* had somehow managed to miss a cluster of rocks and had run directly up onto the beach in such a way that only the aft part of his boat was still afloat, with its bow securely wedged into the sand.

Evidently, Tumbleweed had so much to drink that he did not realize he had run his boat straight into the island and was in fact beached. At this point I was as close to the beach as the water depth would allow. Being larger, the Coast Guard boat was a little further out and asked me on the radio if I could see or smell gasoline, which I could not. With collisions and hard groundings, leaking fuel is both an environmental hazard and a fire hazard. There were two larger fire department boats and one 20-foot police/harbormaster boat now coming on scene. The police boat came alongside and asked if I had seen or talked to Tumbleweed.

I replied, "Yes, he said he was frightened of the boat sinking with him on it, and I watched him as he jumped off the boat into knee deep water. Tumbleweed is presently sitting on the beach and still wearing his lifejacket. Given his slurred speech and actions, I suspect he may have been drinking." The police boat with two armed officers on board approached the beach and escorted Tumbleweed into their boat. When

Rescue Boat

they came close by me on the way out, Tumbleweed was sitting in the stern of the police boat and was wearing handcuffs.

Epilogue. Because Tumbleweed was a member of a different rescue boat service, and the boat was not leaking fluids or in danger of sinking, the Coast Guard called Tumbleweed's rescue boat service, told them there was no leaking fluids or danger of sinking, and suggested they wait until daylight to refloat the boat. My job was done, so I was able to return to base, dock my boat, and go home after another long day on the water.

Captain's Note: Boating under the influence (BUI) is as dangerous on the water as a DUI in a motor vehicle on land. Captain Bob and I have both seen many near and actual disasters, including serious boat wrecks and underway collisions, caused by too much drinking, or on occasion, illegal drug use. The practice of appointing a designated and nondrinking driver should be a must for all boaters who intend to party. Please keep in mind that our goal in telling these stories, which we hope are instructive as well as entertaining, is safety for the boat operator, for his or her passengers, and for others he or she may encounter on the water.

Episode 19

Captain's Log: *Boats, Rafts, Snakes, and Ramps*

Captain Robert Behling

In this episode, "Boats, Rafts, Snakes, and Ramps," Captain Bob moves inland for his stories: #1 "Rafting in the Salmon River," #2 "Sightseeing on the Snake River," #3 "Boat Balancing Acts," #4 "Snakes in South Carolina," and #5 "Rusty Trucks." When you lead an active lifestyle, unexpected things happen, often out of your control. These stories illustrate situations experienced during everyday outings and remind us what might happen on any given boating adventure.

We have all had events occur that were unplanned, and often they had serious impact on our daily lives. These events are usually simple, short lived, and may not warrant development as an episode so we present them as a collection of stories in a single episode. But they do each have an important message that is worth remembering. I have compiled some events that I have encountered during my life, or stories that have been shared by friends. The events contained in this episode include rafting in the Salmon River, shear pins in the Snake River, boat balancing acts, snakes in South Carolina, and rusty trucks. Each contains a lesson for boaters. I am sure that you, our readers, could provide many more.

#1. Rafting on the Salmon River. Boaters know that when you are on the water you have to carry certain items at all times: small hand tools, spare fuel and oil, the odd part such as a shear pin that might fail and cause a breakdown, drinking water, and each of us have other items to add. In preparing for a rafting trip on the Salmon River, Idaho where we would be floating a river through virgin forests and away from civilization for a week, I tried to think of everything I would need to be comfortable and safe. I almost got it right!

Rescue Boat

For this excursion there were 24 passengers and six boatmen, each captaining a four-passenger inflatable rubber raft rigged with a center metal frame with a seat and oarlocks for the boatman to maintain steering and boat control. Two passengers rode up front, two in the stern. Off we went from the launch point, our last view of civilization for the next week. Towards the end of the first day we were having a great time in very swift water with lots of Class 4 rapids. Class 4 rapids include very swift water over a shallow river base with lots of large boulders and obstructions to create swirling currents. They also include waterfalls of several feet, giving rubber rafts the chance to become airborne. This is what we came for!

I was in the front of the raft with my teenage son and noticed one of the tubes was getting a little soft. As we approached a six-foot waterfall the raft became airborne and sailed over, dropped, and dug the nose in as we hit the river and it folded back, smacking me directly in the face. Ouch! More importantly it smashed my glasses beyond repair. I had a safety strap on them, but unfortunately, I did not have another pair. The next six days were somewhat a blur, and I did not get to fully enjoy the river and mountain scenery until the photos we took were later developed and printed.

Story #1 Epilogue. The moral of the story is that you never know what might happen, and you need to be aware of critical items that require redundancy, just in case. We did not have anything go overboard, but it could happen, so essential items like medication should also be redundant and stored in separate locations. Later during the trip, we did have one raft capsize in rough water, and some gear was lost overboard. Fortunately, it was not our raft that overturned.

#2. Sightseeing on the Snake River, Idaho. One lovely Saturday afternoon I decided to take my family on an outing on the Snake River in

Idaho. At the time I had a 14-foot aluminum boat pushed by a 10-horse out-board motor. While motoring down the river and enjoying the scenery I hit a submerged log and broke the shear pin on the prop, as it is supposed to do with a collision. Three kids and a wife on a small boat in a fast-moving river with no engine power could be a recipe for trouble. Fortunately, I was pre-pared with both a paddle and spare shear pin. I paddled towards shore, found a bit of quiet water, and tied up to a tree. It was a little tricky taking off the prop and replacing the pin, but the repair went well, and I was soon on my way. The joy had gone out of the trip, however, so I headed back to the launch point, put the boat on the trailer, and called it a day.

Story #2 Epilogue. The moral of the story is that you need to have hand tools, spare parts, and a means of propulsion if your motor fails. It is also important to know how to make small on-the-water repairs such as replacing the shear pin. While this might seem like common sense, I have seen many boaters who were not adequately prepared for an unplanned event.

#3. Boat Balancing Acts. Lesson: Weight Distribution. My fa-ther was a golfer, not a boater, but he knew his kids loved being on the water, so he purchased and put on a mooring a heavy 17-foot tri-hull with a 25-horsepower outboard. I am sure the boat salesman told him this was a perfect boat for young people as it was very stable and seaworthy. We thought it was a great upgrade from our wooden 12-foot rowboat. On a day when the family was all gathered for a day on the water, us boys took over the boating responsibilities. Unfortunately, we had not yet had basic high school physics, and when everyone wanted to sit in the bow to get a better view as we motored along, why not.

Along came a rogue wave, and we discovered the why not when the bow went up the wave, then dug in on the down slide and we shipped onboard about 100 gallons or more of seawater. Fortunately, no one in the bow was thrown from the boat, but we did have some hurry up bail-ing to get the weight out of the hull and stay afloat.

Story #3 Epilogue. The moral of this story is to watch the distri-bution of weight in your watercraft, especially passengers clustered together. Weight on the bow is the most dangerous, as that is where the driving force of the engine is, and also usually where the least amount of flotation lift is, given the narrowness of the bow, so if the bow is low to the water it is all too easy to put it underwater should you encounter a larger than usual wave. We were lucky and recovered and got the water out of the boat. It may not always turn out that way as with the many heartbreaking disasters in third world countries, where it is not unusual for entire ferryboats to roll over because passengers all move to one side of the ship to get a better view of some event. Weight distribution is a key consideration in naval engineering where supertankers and ships transporting liquids are built with swash bulkheads, essentially walls with holes internal to the tanks to prevent whatever liquid is being carried from moving rapidly side to side. If you enjoy shipboard cruises, or not, you might ask yourself exactly how seaworthy many of these top-heavy looking vessels really are even with their underwater stabilizers. We all know they are not very good at containing viruses.

#4. Snakes in South Carolina. Lesson: Putting on the Brakes. This story is about a couple of friends fishing on the Santee-Cooper River in South Carolina in a 16-foot aluminum boat. They were basically drift fishing, only using their motor to provide some steering when needed. Fishing had been good, and the cooler was filling up. Coming around a point in the river the boat got caught up in some turbulent swift water and started to swing around towards shore just as they went under a heavy limb of a tree. Thinking they could control the boat by grabbing the limb, one of the men reached up, grabbed hold, and the motion of the boat put pressure on the limb and shook it. Unfortunately, there was a cottonmouth resting on the limb, and it fell directly at their feet onto the boat deck. There was a mad scramble to avoid the snake, and they ultimately turned the boat over trying to get away from this very poisonous reptile.

They managed to wade on shore and catch a

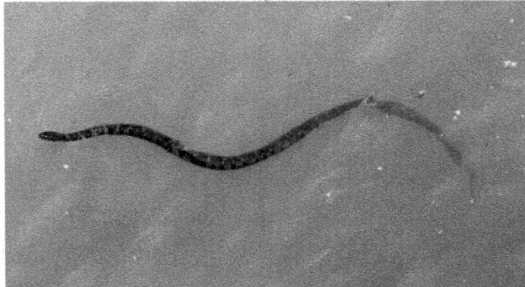

line to secure their boat to the tree, but their fishing gear and catch was lost and floating downriver, never to be found. A memorable but disappointing fishing trip.

Story #4 Epilogue. The moral of the story is be careful what you grab and where you place your feet and hands. Over the years, especially when I fished the high desert lakes of the western states, rattlesnakes were always a concern. They loved to avoid the heat of the day inside an outhouse, under a trash receptacle, or under your vehicle or trailer. I have also seen them swimming in the lakes, and I even had one come up to my boat and try to climb aboard. Situational awareness is very important and could save you from a world of hurt. At the risk of being too "preachy," situational awareness is a lot like knowing where you are. On a boat everything is in motion: the boat, the water, the wind, all the people, and other boats. Like knowing where you are, an experienced captain is constantly alert to all these things and over time develops an innate sense of when all is well, and more importantly, when it is not.

#5. Rusty Trucks. As I was preparing for a move from Cape Cod to the west coast of Florida, my brother called and asked what I planned to do with my pickup truck. It had given great service towing my boat for eight years, but my new home had a dock with a boat lift and gulf access, so I no longer needed to trailer it. He said if I was not going to take it with me, he could use it as he was helping one of his girls do some home renovation projects. So, I gave it to him. About a month later I got a call late one afternoon, and the first thing I heard was my brother saying, "That free truck has turned out to be the most expensive free truck I have ever owned!"

Naturally I asked him what he was talking about. He said he was sitting on the side of the road with a load of building materials on board. The salt water from all my boat launchings (many Cape Cod ramps are shallow drop-offs, so you have to put the rear axle in the water to float the boat) had corroded the brake lines and connections to the wheel cylinders, causing a leak in the line and ultimately the loss of brake fluid. When he applied the brakes to avoid a squirrel nothing happened! The truck had manual shifting, so he was able to downshift and bring it to a stop safely. This was not a problem you could fix alongside the road, and he was waiting for a tow truck.

Story #5 Epilogue. The moral of the story is to remember to look where it is not obvious for maintenance issues. I checked my trailer regularly, but never thought to crawl under the truck and see what had rusted. It was fortunate that I was not towing my boat when it happened, it could have been a bad scene. Motor vehicles and saltwater are arch enemies. As this story relates, salt water literally erodes steel over time. The best prevention is, as they say when referring to another fun activity, abstention. Keeping your tow vehicle out of salt water is key. How can you manage this? Maybe by using a roller instead of bunk trailer, by using a trailer with a longer tongue, or better yet, finding a launch ramp with a steeper slope.

Florida, for example, has mastered the art of boat ramps. Nearly all have a steep enough incline to launch and haul without putting the tow vehicle in the water, and best of all is that many ramps have two different slopes, the nearest part being less steep and the further being steeper. These work especially well. In Florida there are usually two to six ramps in any given location, supported by ample and well-designed docks, trailer parking, clean heads, and last but not least, fish cleaning stations. I have even seen boat washing stations at some of these ramps. Given today's cost of boats, towing vehicles, and docking, it would seem that having well designed, well-built, and well located ramps is a sure way to ensure public access to waterways and support boaters and the boating industry that brings jobs and tourists to every state. Judging from the condition and limited number of boat ramps open to the public, it is evident that many northeastern states, or at least their political representatives who control funding, do not share this view.

Episode 20
Captain's Log: *Navigating Blind*
Captain Hal Records

In Episode 20 we return to the rescue boat business and to the seacoast of New England to test our understanding of navigation and navigational instruments. This episode relates the tales of two separate marine situations: "Navigating Blind #1" as managed from Rescue Boat Dispatch; and "Navigating Blind #2", a story of survival at sea.

***Captain's Log. 20: 30 hours, Tuesday September 7.* "Navigating Blind #1."** It had been a pleasantly quiet day at Rescue Boat Dispatch as the chaos of last week's Labor Day weekend was past. The kids were all back in school, obviously in the pre-Covid years, and many boaters were planning for season end haul-outs so we were enjoying the first relative lapse in daily runs since Memorial Day in May. This boating season wasn't over, but it was on the wane. The boss, Keith had taken the day off, a highly unusual event, so Captain Mark and I were on duty in dispatch enjoying some storytelling and a last minute cup of coffee before the anticipated 21:00 end of our shifts. As mentioned previously, Rescue Boat never closes. At the end of each day the last person out walks down to the dock and checks that all the rescue boats are securely tied, fueled, and electronics turned off. Upon returning to the office they turn off computer screens, forward the phone to whomever has the night watch, turn off the lights, lock the door, and put the cat out... oops, we don't really have a cat.

True to form, on this night the telephone rang at 20:45 and a representative of Geico Insurance (not the little green gecko) politely asked, "How long will it take you to get a tow truck to 24 Mainstreet in Warren where a customer of ours has broken down?"

We still get at least two or three calls similar to this every week. Our standard response is, "Sir, this is Rescue Boat towing. We tow boats.

Rescue Boat

Sorry, but we do not tow automobiles unless they are in or under the water." The agent did not seem to think that was funny. At 20:50 another call came in...

Captain's Log. 20:50 hours, Tuesday September 7. The caller sounded like a middle-aged lady, let's call her Alzda. She and her husband Larry were returning to Newport from a Labor Day voyage to Nantucket aboard their 40-foot Carver yacht. Larry was piloting and they were both on the bridge.

My response was, "This is Rescue Boat Dispatch Rhode Island, how may I help you?"

Alzada said it was nearly dark and very foggy where they were in southwestern Buzzards Bay, Massachusetts, and that they were low on fuel. She asked how long it would take them to get to Newport, and if they had enough fuel.

Before answering her question I needed several pieces of information starting with—you guessed it—exactly where are you, followed by what is your course and speed, what are your fuel gauge readings and are you diesel or gasoline powered? At that relatively large size, I was pretty sure they were diesel powered, and I also knew that such a boat would carry about 350 gallons of fuel. Her fuel economy would be about 1 mile per gallon so that at 15 knots, 21 miles per hour she would consume about 21 gallons of fuel per hour.

Now for the missing variables, I asked, "Where are you so I can calculate the distance and fuel required to get from your present location to Newport, and what are your current fuel gauge readings to see if you have enough fuel to make it." When calculating fuel requirements for a voyage, the standard is to use one fourth of your fuel to get where you are going, one fourth to use while you are at your destination, one fourth of your fuel to get back home, and one fourth of your fuel for reserve. It is neither wise nor safe to undercut this guideline because fuel use can vary markedly due to weather and sea conditions, navigation accuracy, speed of the vessel, and the number of passengers and weight aboard at any given time.

When asked for their speed Alzada replied 15 knots, when asked for fuel levels she said just over one quarter tank, so far so good, when asked where they were she said, "I don't know Larry doesn't have the GPS on."

They were **navigating blind.** My mental response was unprintable but my oral response was, "Please put Captain Larry on the phone," which she did. I then asked Captain Larry to please turn on his GPS, which he did.

Captain's Log. 21:00 hours, Tuesday September 7. I also asked Captain Larry for the course he was steering. Once I got his lat/long and course I could see we had a real problem. "Captain Larry, shut your engines down RIGHT NOW!"

His response was, "Why should I do that?"

My answer: "Because you will be on the rocks at Sakonnet Point in five minutes if you do not." OOPS. Visibility at Rescue Base up in the bay was good, but there was a cold front moving in from offshore that left Captain Larry's visibility at about 100 feet. At 15 knots he would never even have been able to see the rocks before crashing into them, with disastrous results. Captain Larry could now see his location on his own GPS, and I could hear a muttered "Holy sh- -" in the background. I was looking at the same setting on a navigational computer screen in the dispatch office. After a quick calculation, my next statement to Captain Larry was to set a new course and steer 180 degrees for 10 minutes at 10 knots.

His response was, "Why, that course will take me straight to sea and away from the coast."

My response: "Yes it will take you about two miles offshore, and from that point on you will need to call me every 15 minutes so I can verify your location and provide course changes as needed. This way you can also avoid an area of miles long fish traps located near the Sakonnet River and seaward of the Newport beaches, all of which are between you and your destination." He obviously knew nothing about the fish traps, which are serious risks to navigation.

All of a sudden Captain Larry became less argumentative and more willing to accept advice. I estimated that the Carver had about 90 gallons of fuel aboard and that he could make Newport on about 45 gallons, hence there was no need to dispatch a rescue boat to tow him in. Had a rescue boat been required it would have been a long tow because the 10 gallons of diesel carried on the towboat for emergencies would barely cover the bottom of his fuel tank, let alone power two big engines for any distance.

Rescue Boat

Captain's Log. 22:30 hours, Tuesday September 7. Captain Larry called in regularly every 15 minutes as directed and I could see on my electronic charts that he was making good progress. When he finally called only five minutes since his preceding call he said that he and Alzada had just cleared the fog, the visibility was crystal clear, and he could see the lights of Newport Harbor about two miles ahead. He and especially Alzada thanked me for getting them safely into port.

Epilogue. At Rescue Boat, many times our best and most successful service to clients is when we don't even dispatch a boat, or get out on the water. As in this case of blind navigation we were able to prevent what could have been a disaster without ever leaving the office. I switched the phones over, closed the office, and went home. That night it took a little extra time to unwind before I could sleep. I kept visualizing in my mind some of the boats I have seen over the years that have smashed onto rocks. Many were what we call "chainsaw salvages," or vessels so severely damaged that they had to be cut into pieces and removed with land based construction equipment.

Captain's Log. 20:30 hours, Tuesday September 7. "Navigating Blind #2." I had just completed a jumpstart in the New Harbor Block Island, which is 14 miles out from the southern rescue boat base in Point Judith. The call had come in at about 19:30 as I was returning to base from another run, so it had only taken half an hour to get out to the island. The vessel needing a jumpstart was a 34-foot Sea Ray. Her captain, let's call him Ivan, and crew had gone ashore for an afternoon tour of the island and dinner at the Oar Restaurant. Most boats of this size have at least two batteries or even battery banks. One battery is considered to be for engine starting and the other a "house battery" for things like a refrigerator, TVs, stereos, and air conditioning. These batteries are connected to a switch that toggles between Battery 1, Battery 2, Both, Off, and Shore Power. The normal practice upon docking is to plug in a special electrical cable from the dock and switch to shore power. If on a mooring the normal practice once the boat is securely moored is to toggle the switch to whichever battery is the house battery. This way if a battery should go flat, it does not impact the starting or running of the vessel's engines, which is particularly important because running the engines is what charges all the batteries. Some larger boats and many long range cruisers have independent gas or diesel operated generators for this purpose, and hence very seldom need a jumpstart.

As it turns out, Captain Ivan did not toggle his batteries and inadvertently left the air conditioning and some lights turned on when they boarded the launch for their adventure ashore. Needless to say, when they returned to the boat at dark they had no lights and could not start their engines, hence the call to Rescue Boat. Ivan was a Rescue Boat member so although there was no charge for the jumpstart, he did pass me a nice tip, which is never solicited but always appreciated.

Captain's Log. 21:30 hours. The weather had been deteriorating all afternoon. What started out as a five knot wind (my favorite speed) from the east had by now swung up to the northeast and was cranking.

The weather forecast was for 20 knots, heavy rain, and localized thunderstorms, so I did not dawdle after completing the jumpstart, but immediately headed out the channel and swung northwest toward home port. I was again on Rescue Boat Three, the 23-foot Steiger, and I really did not want a repeat of the events in Episode 11, "Keep the Open Side Up." About halfway across the open ocean between Block Island and Point Judith the weather took a nasty turn for the worse. Yeah, localized thunderstorms all right. Seas were only four to five feet, but there was a nasty chop on top of the ground swells. This chop was breaking over Rescue Three's starboard gunnel and into the cockpit over her relatively shallow sides. I had cleverly not put up her isinglass side panels so I was pretty much soaked to the skin.

The wind was 20 knots and I was running into it at about 15 knots; that translates to rain and sea coming aboard the starboard side at about 35 knots. On a night like this, a really nice feature of little Rescue Boat Three, as shown in this picture, is that she has scuppers on steroids.

Rescue Boat

These are two six-inch diameter fire hoses attached to her oversized scuppers such that when the hoses are in the down position as shown here, the forward motion of the boat causes the scuppers to behave like big pumps sucking a great deal of water out of the cockpit and thereby keeping the boat afloat. In the photo you can see a white line on each side of the transom that extends from a cam cleat on each gunnel to the outboard end of the fire hose.

Also note the motor guard mounted on the transom of the boat that protects the engines and keeps the tow hawser, which runs from the aft bollard and over the guard, from fouling the propellers. This, the shape of the hull, and the reliability of her two Suzuki 140 horsepower engines is why Rescue Boat Three, although small, *always brings us home*. This is a really good attribute for a rescue boat, or any boat for that matter. But I digress ....

Captain's Log. 22:00 hours. At this point, soaking wet, in nasty seas and in the middle of severe thunderstorm my GPS went out. Ok, it didn't really go out, the screen just went all fuzzy and looked like the wrong end of a sheep. No problem; my 24 mile Furuno radar is bulletproof so I can still see where land is, about seven miles to the west. Then, you guessed it, a really funny thing happened and the Furuno radar went all fuzzy and looked like the inside of a blizzard. Ok, time to take inventory. I was now **navigating blind**. What if the wind changed direction and I was steaming to sea instead of toward shore? Do you have any idea how dark and lonely it is out in the ocean in rough seas with lightning flashing, thunder rolling, and large quantities of salt water splashing in over the side of your boat, especially when you don't really know which way the land is?

The first step was to hold course, hence to keep the starboard bow into the sea, and hold speed to keep the aforementioned scuppers working and most of the water out of the boat. The second step that rescue boat captains take is to telephone or radio dispatch to tell them where you are, or at least your last known position, and what your situation is. That way they can get your epitaph right...not really.

As always when rescue boats are on the water in challenging conditions, Captain Keith, the boss, is in dispatch to back you up, as he was this night. His first comment in a deadpan voice was, "Gee Hank, funny night for a boat ride, what are you doing out there?" He knew damn well what I was doing out there. He then told me to hold course and speed and that according to his radar, this severe cell would pass beyond me in about 10 minutes, after which I should reboot the GPS and it would come up. He then said that the surface spray was confusing my radar and it would come back on its own soon after the GPS, once the wind stopped chopping off the tops of the waves. So I did, and it did, and little Rescue Boat Three cleared the west passage breakwater into the Point Judith Harbor of Refuge at about 22:30 hours, none the worse for wear. Although I can't say the same about her captain that night.

Epilogue. These two stories describe **navigating blind**, which is a challenge on a good day. It seems that too many boaters who have grown up with today's sophisticated GPS, depth sounder/fish finder, and radar electronics with large sunlight visible multifunction screens may have become overly dependent on them. As a matter of safety, boats should carry a compass, even a handheld compass is better than none. It may not take you exactly where you want to go, but it will enable you to distinguish east from west and hence sea from shore in the case of an emergency. Likewise, in the interest of safety, captains should at the very least be comfortable with basic dead reckoning navigation which is essentially how to use a compass and traditional charts.

Part 3
Getting Seasoned

Episode 21

Captain's Log: *Gone Fishin'*

Captain Robert Behling

In this episode, "Gone Fishin," Captain Bob switches our focus from rescue mode to sportsman and angler mode, and reminds us why we enjoy boats and boating: we like to have fun on the water and we like to catch fish! Captain Bob has traveled the world, and whenever possible he takes the opportunity to wet a line, or at least share some fishing stories with others. The eight stories told here range from chasing striped bass and bluefish on Cape Cod, ice fishing in Idaho, salmon fishing in Alaska, grappling with a huge grouper in Australia, to arguing with a snapping turtle in Alabama. When reading these stories Captain Hal was reminded of the sign over the front entrance of his local Bass Pro Shop: *"The Place for Fishermen and Other Liars."*

#1 A Near Miss. I was living on Cape Cod, a unique spit of sand that has something to harvest from the sea every month of the year. This was late spring, the weather was sunny and warm, and there was no wind. The blooms on the forsythia told me that the striped bass were due back for their summer visit to Cape Cod after wintering in the warmer southern waters The old timers always used nature to time their fishing efforts. I decided to take my 17-foot Del Quay Dory offshore for a try at catching one. I hooked up my trailer, drove to the launch, and put in without incident.

Where I lived on the Cape, we had a barrier sandbar separating a large bay from the Atlantic, with a cut about 400 yards wide giving access to the ocean that can be challenging at times, especially in a small craft. This day I motored right through the cut without any problems and started my search for fish. One surefire sign that there are fish feeding is a flock of birds diving for the scraps of menhaden floating to the surface after being cut up by feeding fish. It took a while, but I finally spotted some gulls and terns diving. As I got closer, the water looked like a highly active washing machine on the high-speed cycle. The fish and menhaden were near the surface, and it was quite a sight as the bass drove the menhaden into a frenzy. I was rigged with a surf plug, a Bomber Long A, so I tossed it into the melee and immediately had a strike. It was a good size fish and gave me quite a fight. After about 15 minutes I was able to boat a beautiful and very large striped bass. In the meantime, I had drifted away from the feeding school, the birds had dispersed, and it looked like the feeding frenzy may have been over.

I got out my tape and measured the fish. At the time the minimum legal limit for striped bass was 36 inches, which translates into a fish at or over 15 pounds. My measure was clear, 35 ¾ inches. No amount of manipulation would release that last quarter inch that I needed to be legal. Oh well, the fight the fish gave me was exhilarating, and I had some leftover clam chowder for dinner, so while I wanted a fish dinner, I also wanted to stay within the regulations. The fish went over the side of the boat and back into the water to fight on another day. That was one of the larger fish I have ever wanted to keep but decided to release. I don't regret obeying the regulations, but I will always remember the close call I had for a great grilled bass dinner that day.

#2 A Bluefish Field Goal. Most summer mornings I woke up at dawn, checked the weather and wind, and if it was a nice day, I would throw my fishing gear in the back of the truck and head for the beach. There is something very peaceful about standing on the sand watching the sun come up while tossing a plug for bass and/or bluefish. This morning I had a hankering for a breakfast of blackened blue, small snapper blues dusted with Paul Proudhome blackening seasoning, fried in a hot skillet. I knew where they had been catching 14 to 16-inch snapper blues, the perfect size. There is a small sandy beach on a causeway, with a fast drop-off to about 10 feet of water within casting range, and that is where I was headed. I took lightweight gear, as it is more fun to catch snappers when they have a chance to put up a fight.

I made a dozen casts with no action; when I threw the next time I got slammed! At first, I thought it was a nice snapper, but soon watched the line peel off my reel regardless of how much drag I applied, and I knew I had something bigger. The problem with catching something bigger at this location is that there are anchored boat moorings starting at about 30 feet offshore. Crossing lines with them is a surefire way to break off a fish. So, I waded out as far as I could and successfully maneuvered the fish around all the obstacles. I kept the fish off the mooring lines, but the strain on my drag and gears finally caught up to my lightweight equipment and it was starting to fail. Fortunately, the fish was tiring, and I was able to carefully lead it towards the beach. When I saw what was on my line I knew I had been lucky, it was a large bluefish over 15 pounds, and I was using 10-pound test line. The fish glided into water about two feet deep, realized that it was being caught, and gave a mighty lunge. *Snap!* The line broke and the fish was free but was played out, and just laid there for a minute. You do not grab a bluefish with your hands if you want to keep your fingers—their teeth are like razors—so I did the only thing that came to mind. I put my foot under it and gave the fish a mighty kick, and sent it sailing about 20 feet onto the beach. I heard some clapping, turned around, and saw a game warden standing beside her truck.

She told me she saw a fight from the roadway and stopped to watch, fascinated that I could land such a large fish on essentially a trout outfit. She likened my landing technique to kicking a field goal, and said it was good for three bluefish points. She also said she knew of no fish and game regulations that applied to this unusual fish landing technique, and it was the first bluefish field goal she had ever witnessed! I took the fish home and it measured 35 inches, large for a bluefish. I filleted it, and we had smoked bluefish for dinner that evening. The spinning reel that I had been using for the fight was destroyed. I opened it up to see if it could be fixed and all the gears were stripped!

#3 *Alaska, Where the Fish Are.* The fishing scene moves from Cape Cod to Juneau, Alaska. My son-in-law and I were trolling with friends for salmon, and it had been a slow day. Salmon are easy to catch but often hard to find. We rounded a point and three rods had strikes at the same time. Fortunately, they were all good hookups and we landed all three fish. We quickly had one more strike and landing, and then it went dead. I have learned over the years that when you get hookups you turn around and cover the same water again; fish tend to school and it is usually productive to fish the water a second or even a third time. The captain, who was not a very experienced fisherman (he grew up and worked until retirement in Phoenix, Arizona) and our host for the week trolled on a bit with no action, then said he had heard that there were fish at a spot about a mile further on. He did not like anyone challenging his decisions, so I bit my tongue. I so wanted to run that stretch again, but I was not in charge.

That afternoon we landed at the dock with four salmon. The remainder of the day had not been productive. Enough fish for dinner, but not a particularly good catch by Alaskan standards. It was hard to keep still, but it was his boat and he was the Alaska resident, so I told myself to shut up and deal with it! The next day we asked if we could try for halibut, and he said sure, he knew some good halibut water. It turned out he did, and we patiently waited after a 20 mile run to his "favorite spot" while he had his eye glued to the depth finder and moved the boat to be in exactly 400 feet of water, which he firmly believed was just right for halibut at that spot of ocean. He was right on, and within a couple of hours we limited out and came home with some very nice 20-pound fish.

Upon reflection, fishing is more than just catching fish; it is the experiences, the friendships, the scenery, and sometimes the thrill of landing a big one. We had a great week fishing Alaska, I got to spend some quality time with my son-in-law, we made some wonderful memories, and we each came home with a 50-pound container of prime frozen fillets. Who could ask for anything more?

#4 Ice Fishing, Man against Nature. I was living in Idaho, where spring, summer, and fall fishing for both trout and bass is outstanding. But when winter rears its ugly head, fishing comes to a standstill. Not quite, there is something called ice fishing. I had no experience with ice fishing when one day I was offered the opportunity to join a par-

ty headed for one of the mountain lakes to fish through the ice. Why not, I thought, a new adventure doing something I had never done before. The first thing I learned was that you need special gear for ice fishing, both for the fishing and for the fisherman. I borrowed the fishing gear but was totally unprepared for what I was going to find when I got on the lake. I thought I was dressed warmly. NO! I might have been OK sitting on the bank, but out on the ice where there was nothing to break the wind, it was COLD! And we were bucket fishing; that means you drill a hole, set up your rig, and sit on a bucket waiting for a bite. No shanty, no canvas windbreak, nothing to protect you from the ever-present wind roaring down the lake valley. Naturally, it was sub-zero weather that day and I froze my buns off sitting on a darn bucket! I had been cold before when fishing cool fall weather, but I always warmed up when the bite was on! The slow bite and roaring wind taught me a lesson that day.

We didn't have much luck, and I was thankful that our vehicle had an adequate heater to warm us up on the trip home. I could accept that we would probably have hotdogs instead of fried trout for dinner that night. I could not accept that I shivered most of the time on the ice and much of the way home. When asked what I thought about ice fishing, my immediate reply was, "After you did it once, why would you ever do it again?" And I never have.

Fortunately, I now live in Lower Alabama where there is no winter ice, so there is no ice fishing available to tempt me to give it another try. Captain Hal on the other hand did ice fishing on ponds in Connecticut when growing up, and remembers it fondly and although he might not admit it, he now lives and fishes in southern Florida every winter. Perhaps ice fishing is best suited to children with their higher metabolism!

#5 *Competing with an Orvis Guide.* I am back on the Cape Cod causeway beach mentioned in an earlier story. My son had flown in from his home in Florida for some fishing, and after a quick breakfast we headed down to the beach as dawn was breaking, promising a beautiful morning.

We started casting lures for whatever fish might be hanging around in the harbor that would bite. I knew there were juvenile striped bass in the bay and harbors, usually running about 16 to 18 inches and well below the 24-inch legal limit at that time, but fun to catch. We arrived at the causeway beach and were admiring the sunrise. Our lures were doing the trick and we were catching fish with some regularity when a truck pulled up and a well decked out "Orvis" guide and his angler got out and came down to the beach. They saw we were getting strikes so they came within about 30 yards of us and the guide started instructing the angler. In the meantime, we continued catching school bass and throwing them back. They were catching nothing. I knew the reason why.

There was a small piece of structure directly in front of us; the rest of the bottom was sand. I know this because I fished the same spot for flounder in the fall and lost gear on the structure from time to time. I think it might have been the remains of a sunken boat. I could see the angler's frustration increasing, why were these two catching fish and he was paying a guide and getting skunked? Finally, the angler leaned over to the guide and in a loud whisper asked, "What more should I do to catch a fish?"

The guide, again in a loud whisper, leaned over and gave the best instructions I have ever heard in a situation like this: "Move closer to them!" So much for hiring an expensive guide with intimate knowledge of the local fishing. When someone nearby is catching fish and you are not, poach their spot if you can! That says it all. I should note that I call guides who wear special vests with all kinds of tools and equipment hanging on clips "Orvis guides" and do not mean to imply that they actually work for Orvis, only that they probably buy their vest and displayed gear from Orvis. By the way, if you are not familiar with Orvis, they sell very high-quality products and fishing equipment. I own some myself.

Shortly after the conversation between the guide and angler we packed up and headed home, leaving them our choice spot. I don't know if our moving on helped the angler catch fish or not. Perhaps it did help the guide be more successful the next time he took an angler to fish the causeway beach! For us, the sun was up, the tide was out, and it was time to think about harvesting some clams for lunch.

Rescue Boat

#6 A Really Big One is Getting Away! My children were grown and off pursuing their own careers, giving me some options for deciding how I wanted to spend my time. I was talking with a friend who had just returned from completing a six month teaching contract in Australia, and she extoled the virtues of the experience: the beauty of the landscape, the people, the outback, and the city life she found in Sydney. She encouraged me to give it a try, and she would help grease the skids for me if I wanted to pursue getting a contract. I did, and I was able to successfully negotiate a six-month contract, so I packed up and ventured off to work in Wollongong, New South Wales. The university where I would be teaching arranged for a condo near the beach, and several times a week I would venture down to the water to see what was happening. One Saturday I was walking along a rocky point and I spotted a fisherman, so of course I had to stop and talk. He was a market fisherman targeting grouper for the restaurant trade and came to this spot to fish most Saturdays.

The fisherman told me that he had no catch that morning and as we talked, he related a story worth sharing. He was fishing this same spot a few months before and had hooked up with a large fish. He said he was carefully playing it for about half an hour when he finally got a look at it. It was a huge grouper, over 200 pounds. What a payday if he could get it on the shore! A fish that big generally controls the situation, and this one did as well. Some of the fight had gone out of it after the long struggle, but it is not over until it is over.

Several feet short of a successful landing the fish managed to break off, dashing the fisherman's dreams of extra cash that weekend. He told me he made an instant decision, put down his fishing pole, and jumped into the water. He grabbed the fish around the gill area and wrestled it up onto the beach. Fortunately, the fish was tired out, or it might have put up more of a struggle and put him in danger of something bad happening. Instead, after delivering the fish to the Sydney marketplace, he had a nice wad of cash in his pocket and was able to fish on for another day.

I have often thought of this encounter and subsequent story, and while I was more than willing to give the bluefish I had break off a good swift kick, I don't know if I would get into the water and risk life and limb to tackle a 200 pound monster grouper.

Captain Hal tells the tale of another giant grouper; this one happened while he was serving in the US Navy in the late 1960s and was stationed in the Philippines. He was scuba diving in a lagoon near a coral reef, and as he returned to the dive boat, he saw a giant piece of mushroom shaped coral. Next to this was a dark shape, certainly not a shark, but thick and tall and long…and moving ever so slowly away as Captain Hal swam down for a closer look. He followed the fish down the side of the reef from a depth of about 50 feet to nearly 90 feet but did not have enough air left in his dive tank to pursue further. The massive fish appeared to be a grouper about 12 feet long and nearly six feet tall. Captain Hal immediately realized this was an incredible opportunity to view a fish you might only see once in a lifetime, and he returned to the dive boat knowing that the sea does indeed hold magical wonders.

Fortunately, my biggest catch ever, a 96-inch blue marlin caught trolling off the coast of Hilo, Hawaii stayed hooked up, even after eleven spectacular jumps. Each jump put my heart in my throat, fearful that the line would catch the bill or dorsal fin and break, or the magnificent fish would throw the hook. After a 45-minute fight I managed to land it, thanks to a very skillful captain and crew.

#7 *Setting a Record Fishing the Surf with a Fly Rod.* While living on the Cape I became acquainted with a fellow fisherman who ran a small printshop. Printing was how he paid the rent; his avocation was water-color painting, and he was very good. I purchased many of his seascapes over the years for myself and to give as gifts. He told me that each evening he would come home from the shop, paint for 15 to 20 minutes, and if something good came out, great. If not, toss it and wait until tomorrow for more inspiration. After a quick dinner, if there was enough light, he would head to the beach to do some surf fishing. What made him unusual was his 12-foot fly rod, not something that was easy to handle.

As we became better acquainted, he loosened up and started telling stories of his fishing exploits over the years. One evening stood out in his mind. He was casting a fly into the "suds" (backwash and turmoil from the surf) off one of our popular beaches where the bass often come in and feed on whatever the turbulent water stirs up from the bottom—crabs, clams, worms and the like. He was about ready to give up from lack of action when he got a solid strike. He is no small guy, but this fish put him to the test. It was almost dark when he finally landed it, and he said his eyes bugged out at the sight of the striped bass lying on the sand. He had never caught anything that big before. He iced it down, and when he took it to be weighed the next day it passed the 73-pound mark! What a catch from the surf using a fly rod. He submitted it for a record and told me he was awarded a world record for striped bass on a fly rod with the test weight gear he was using. I can imagine the thrill and excitement he experienced, knowing that he was one of only a select few anglers to ever be recognized with a world record.

#8 Crabby Turtles...Really! I no longer go fishing alone on a boat, so when I get the urge, I often mosey down to a state provided fishing dock on appropriately enough, the Fish River. The river empties into Mobile Bay, which is brackish water but by no means true salt. It does hold redfish, black drum, speckled trout, croaker, and other assorted local species, as well as a good population of shrimp and blue crab. When you fish the dock you just never know what might show up. On one recent early morning outing I decided to both fish and crab, so I put out a line with shrimp for bait and set two drop side crab traps from the dock and threw out two hand lines, all baited with fish bodies. I had previously eaten the fillets, and I could already taste an ice cod crab cocktail with a nice glass of wine with my dinner.

Right off the bat I attracted a crab to one of my further out hand lines and managed to bring it in and net it without having it drop off. This was the start to what I hoped would be a good day crabbing. The shrimp baited pole got a strike next, and it was a

croaker, very good for crab bait so I was satisfied with the catch. The next hour I caught more croaker and crabs which were both attracted by my hand lines and my near dock traps. Then something strange happened.

I was doing a routine pull on my traps and one felt like it caught a branch or had a load of rocks in it. What the heck? I got it up and found I had a snapping turtle as big as half a basketball munching on my fish body bait. I opened the trap on the dock, and he crawled out, not very happy to be out of the water and trapped on a dock. I thought of turtle soup, but how the heck would I get him home to butcher him? Add to that the fact that I have never butchered a turtle and had no idea how to go about it. Also, I thought that snapping turtle probably does not taste good anyway. So, I let him find a ledge and crawl off splashing into the river.

Shortly after the turtle incident I had a crab on one of my handlines and started to retrieve it. Suddenly the line went taught and I felt a huge surge, then nothing. An old timer on the dock looked over and said, "What you had was either a bull redfish or a large black drum, they both like crabs." Whatever it was, my crab and fish body bait were both gone, along with my sinker and shower curtain ring that I use to hold the bait to the line. I will never know what I had for sure, but it brought back a memory from a few years before.

I was fishing from the same dock, and had a heavy pole rigged with a fish body for bait and a heavy sinker out into deep water searching for crabs. The heavy sinker gets the bait down quickly, necessary when pelicans are around trying to grab the fish body when it hits the water. Catching a pelican can lead to trouble, either breaking off or injuring the pelican when you try and dislodge the bait from their bill.

A pod of dolphin came by, something I regularly see in the river as the mature dolphins bring the juveniles into the river to teach them how to fish. Suddenly the line went taut and the drag started screaming. That was no crab! A dolphin had picked up the fish body and was making a run for the bay. After about fifty yards the dolphin surfaced, stood up on its tail and shook its head. *SNAP!* End of story, but the memory remains! What an exciting experience.

Episode 22

Captain's Log: *Live Fire*

Captain Hal Records

This episode begins with an offshore fishing adventure but goes to the heart of safety on the open ocean. Hopefully, the story will strike a familiar chord with all mariners. We begin with a fishing party experiencing the excitement of night fishing for swordfish off the southeast coast of Florida. The details described are based on a story told to me by my good friend Captain Levi Pitman. Captain Levi runs a charter fishing business out of Port Saint Lucie, Florida. He is a young man with a lot of heart and a lot of marine skills beyond finding and catching large fish, including boat and engine repair. He has more tackle and fishing gear than your local bait and tackle shop and has shown exceptional skill and success fishing in deep water and extremely deep water, ranging up to 2,000 feet.

Background. Captain Levi had been looking forward to and planning this swordfishing trip with his friend George for some time. George operates a 25-foot Aquasport center console powered by twin Honda engines and frequently fishes offshore, but not very often for swordfish, which are generally found in 1,000 to 2,000 feet of water. To get to the fishing grounds he needs to travel about 30 miles east from the Saint Lucie Florida Inlet. A prime location for fishing in this area is called the Pumpkin Patch, which is named for the orange, almost salmon color swordfish caught in this area get from a diet high in shrimp. The Pumpkin Patch is located on the 1,000-foot depth line found about 20 miles east northeast of the Saint Lucie Inlet. Other prime fishing spots include the South Hump, North Hump, and Fort Pierce Canyon, which are each about 30 miles out from the inlet. If you are willing to go offshore and travel a bit, there is an abundance of excellent fishing in the area.

Getting Seasoned

The fishery for billfish, including sailfish and swordfish, is so good that Stuart, Florida, with ocean access via the Saint Lucie Inlet, is considered to have some of the best bill fishing in the world. Stuart is recognized as the Sailfish Capital of the World and hosts numerous high yield Billfish tournaments every year. There is even a statue/fountain of a swordfish in downtown Stuart.

Captain's Log 16:00 hours 22 February. This was to be the big day, or rather the big night, since swordfish seem to bite better at night. Captain Levi was loading his heavy duty diesel Dodge Ram with stout tuna rods, high line capacity electric reels and their mini sized 12-volt batteries, nine-pound lead sinkers that look like window sash weights, special small attractor lights to attach to the deep drop rigs near the bait, two big tackle boxes, and of course large coolers packed with ice: one for food and one for bait, much of which had already been rigged with hooks. Offshore bill fishing can be an expensive sport, and it is not unusual for a single day or night fishing trip to ring up costs totaling $500 or more for the basic necessities: ice, bait, tackle, and fuel. Even with these high costs, if the trip is successful the rewards of hooking and landing a giant gamefish can be tremendous.

Captain's Log 17:00 hours 22 February. George and two friends were just pulling into Port Salerno's Sandsprit Park with their trailered boat when Captain Levi arrived. They both parked their vehicles in the staging area and transferred the gear directly from Levi's truck into the boat. This saves the added work of carrying all this stuff from the parking area down to the dock if the boat is launched before loading. As Levi parked, George and his friends launched the boat and organized all the fishing gear. The wind looked to be light from the southwest and the tide was running out. These are perfect conditions and there would be a half moon tonight so not pitch dark, at least until 02:00 or so.

Captain's Log 18:00 hours 22 February. With the boat underway George turned on his VHF radio to Channel 16 just in time to hear a message. "Securite, Securite this is Coast Guard Southeast. All mariners beware; the Coast Guard will be conducting live fire drills near the 30-

mile line between 23:00 and 03:00 hours tonight. All mariners are ad-vised keep clear of a 10-mile radius surrounding this location during those hours. Coast Guard out."

No problem, George and Levi would be fishing 40 miles out in 2,000 feet of water by then and hopefully fighting a big swordfish.

Captain's Log 19:00 hours 22 February. The sun was just set-ting to the west as Levi and company cleared the Saint Lucie Inlet on an east-northeast course and began to follow their GPS directions to the co-ordinates for the swordfishing grounds. Almost everyone headed to sea from the east coast of Florida notices as land disappears in the wake, that the shoreline all looks the same. There are not really any unique or distinc-tive topographical features, and one high rise building looks like every other. At five miles out it is no longer possible to even distinguish the inlet. Returning to the inlet is the same, hence the mariner's navigation needs to be good. On the two-hour run out to the fishing grounds Levi was setting up rods in the appropriate locations on the boat so they could drift fish four rigs at a time, each at a different depth ranging from 200 feet down to 1,000 feet. Each rod would be rigged with an electric reel, two hooks bait-ed with a whole squid, a nine-pound weight, and because it is dark in deep water, a small underwater light to attract attention to the bait.

Captain's Log 01:00 hours 23 February. They had arrived at their destination 40 miles offshore at about 22:00 hours. The lines were baited and set, and all but Levi were sleeping soundly, then a rod bent hard and the reel started to sing. Levi yelled "Fish on!" for the others to wake up and get all the lines in before this fish got tangled in one of them and got away. The reel was screaming, and the heavy rod was bent nearly to the waterline. This was definitely a big fish, and they were in for a long and grueling fight

to land it. Then the Coast Guard live fire exercise started. There were bright flashes to the east, followed by the sound of rapid gunfire echoing across the gentle swell of the two-foot seas. Echoes of gunfire over the water at night are a unique and unnerving sound, even when they are expected.

The fish was still running hard, and George started the engines, flipped on his running lights so he could be easily seen, and began following the fish. Using the boat to chase a hooked fish is a normal procedure when hooked up to a really big fish whether it is a tuna, sailfish, shark, or swordfish. Levi and George had no way of knowing exactly what had latched onto the end their now nearly 900 feet of line. The fish was leading them on a merry chase left and right as they followed, and gradually they were able to retrieve line and get him nearer the boat. First down to 700 feet of line, then 600 and 500 and 400 feet. More echoes of gunfire, some rapid and some more deliberate, but at what seemed to be a safe distance from their current location.

Captain's Log 02:00 hours 23 February. The boat continued to maneuver as the line came in to 300 feet, then 200 feet. If it was a swordfish would it jump? That would be the sight of a lifetime in the moonlight. Everyone was focused on the fish: what was it, would it jump, could they bring it to the boat? Sometime during the excitement, the gunfire had stopped, the live fire exercise must have finished. It was quiet, the line kept coming in, 100 feet, 50 feet, and then a giant bill fish suddenly leaped out of the water, twisted his silver head and long sword, and shook the hook and bait out of his mouth. A loud groan of disappointment emanated from the fishermen.

Almost immediately and quite shockingly the boat was bathed in what appeared to be broad daylight. The decks were lighted from above;

there was a blue flashing light behind the bright white light, a siren wailed, and a big deep spooky voice echoed over a bullhorn.

"This is the US Coastguard Cutter *Ivan Point*. Heave to and prepare to be boarded." Uh-Oh! Did we inadvertently follow the fish into the live fire zone?

Captain's Log 02:30 hours 23 February. Next a bright orange seriously overpowered Coast Guard RIB with a mounted and manned 50 caliber machine gun in the bow appeared from behind the big cutter and pulled alongside our boat. Three heavily armed uniformed Coast Guard crew, two men and one woman, climbed aboard. They did not speak but immediately began looking in every nook, cranny, and container on the boat. They asked if we had weapons aboard and George said no. They asked what we were doing 40 miles offshore in a small boat, and George said, "Fishing, and with some success, at least until you arrived and scared the fish off."

Oops! That was not the answer they were looking for. The young woman who led the boarding party was a chief petty officer and was wearing what appeared to be a nine-millimeter automatic pistol strapped to her right leg. Let's call her Chief.

Levi whispered, "Shut up George! Do not do or say anything that will aggravate the Chief!" after which she said rather curtly, "Okay, no drugs; check the safety gear."

George is a good and safety conscious captain, his safety gear would certainly be all right and it was, except for the expiration date on the 12-gauge signal flares, which were 30 days past expiration. Whew, not a big violation, I have in the past been given a warning for this, but not a citation. Chief had a different solution, I think she really didn't like George's earlier response and she turned and said, "Captain, your fishing trip is over. Gather your gear and return to port immediately." Then she followed her team over the rail into the RIB and headed back to the cutter.

Captain's Note. Outdated signal flares are a common problem. Expiration dates are clearly printed on each flare so check your flares' expiration date now and always check the dates when you purchase new ones. I have seen flares for sale in stores that are already past their expiration dates. It is alright to have outdated flares on your boat so long as you also have unexpired flares onboard. Be aware that flares contain explosive and pyrotechnic ingredients that may break down over time and can be dangerous, so accumulating them over a period of years may be hazardous. Flares must be disposed of as you would dispose of any ammunition, and from time to time most local Coast Guard Auxiliary Flotillas have flare collection days when you can drop them off for safe disposal.

Epilogue. As the large cutter disappeared into the now pitch-dark night, George packed up their gear, set the GPS for home, and headed west, having in mind a little fishing along the way. Unfortunately, the Coast Guard was laying dark just outside their range of vision and as they passed by, the cutter turned on her running lights and followed them all the way back and into Saint Lucie Inlet. While annoyed at having to give up their fishing that night, the fishermen respected the safety conscious intervention of the Coast Guard.

In fairness to the US Coast Guard, offshore drug interdiction is a major activity in south Florida. Small fast boats rendezvous with larger vessels offshore to pick up the "goods" and then speed into whatever inlet is closest at the time. No doubt Captain Levi's fishing expedition weaving in and out while chasing the swordfish looked on radar to be defensive tactics, hence the Coast Guard's interest in boarding. The message to go home was due to the violation with the expired flares, a safety hazard in the event of trouble and the subsequent need to send a distress signal while on the high seas. Sure, the Chief was nitpicking, but in all honesty, she was also right.

Episode 23

Captain's Log: *Fire On Board*

Captain Hal Records

Episode 23, "Fire on Board," returns to northern waters and rescue boat operations to describe and illustrate several dangerous situations created by fire on boats. Fire can cause catastrophic damage to a vessel, and as such deserves special attention from mariners regarding both fire prevention and control. The idea of fire on a boat can be frightening and intimidating. Imagine your boat catching fire, perhaps from faulty wiring, an engine malfunction, cooking practices, a spark too close to a fuel vent, or yes, even persons smoking near flammable products or fumes, which clearly falls into the dumb and dumber category.

The first rule of thumb for any mariner is if your boat is burning out of control, get away from it. Boats can be replaced, lives cannot. Mariners should ask themselves if they have a fire on board, do they have the correct equipment to fight the fire, as well as the requisite skills. If you have passengers onboard, your and their safety needs to be your first concern, starting with immediately getting everyone into a lifejacket. When should you stay and fight the fire, and when should you call a Mayday and/or abandon ship? This is perhaps the most critical decision the captain must make, and usually there is not a lot of time to think about it.

Prologue. Priority one as with all maritime emergencies is human life. Don't risk people's lives to save boats. Always be aware of your surroundings. Are you offshore where rescue services will take longer to get to you? Should you immediately call a Mayday or first try to fight the fire? How long will it take for emergency responders to arrive? Is everyone in a lifejacket? Can you reasonably expect to put the fire out yourself? How long will it take you to answer these questions? With any boat fire, danger one is burning and danger two is drowning.

143

Getting Seasoned

Get everyone in a lifejacket and topside immediately upon discovery of a fire onboard. Should things go seriously bad, get everyone and your ditch bag into the dinghy or at least overboard and away from the boat as quickly as possible. If your boat is burning out of control, get away from it. Fuel tanks can explode and sinking boats can create a vortex that will take people with them to the bottom of the sea.

Fighting boat fires and providing medical attention are very specific skills that require specially trained people and appropriate fire suppression equipment. Good Samaritans and rescue boat captains should and need to help where they can, but as on shore, first responders on the water are far and away the best solution to resolving a fire on board. The US Coast Guard and local fire and police departments are trained to provide this support.

When I first started working for Rescue Boat I was advised that in life threatening situations we should always do whatever we can to save lives and to support first responders, and that in many situations we could provide communications and if necessary rapid transport on the water. At the time I had no idea how sage this advice was. The two stories in this episode are about fire and life-threatening situations on the water. They provide some insight into challenges faced by mariners when confronting an onboard fire, and these situations do not always end well.

Captain's Log. Fire on Board #1. 06:30 hours August 12. I had picked up my morning Dunkin coffee on the way to work and just walked into the Rescue Boat second floor dispatch office. All was quiet. All four rescue boats were lying calmly in their slips. As I always do upon arrival, I switched on the low and high side VHF radios and scanned the bay on this beautiful clear and breezy August morning. Oh damn, right away in the distance on the far side of

the bay I could see a column of deep black smoke roiling up from the surface of the water. Boat fire! I did not wait for the sure to follow Mayday call, but grabbed my go bag, ran down to the docks and jumped into Rescue Boat *Phoenix*, the 26-foot RIB, set her up, turned on the strobe lights, and with throttles firewalled, I headed out into the channel toward the smoke. The VHFs on the boat were on, but curiously there was no Mayday. I was moving at over 30 knots with *Phoenix's* wake running straight and flat behind when the call came in over the VHF, "Mayday, Mayday, Mayday this is *Skipjack*, fire on board, abandoning ship."

Does anyone know the missing piece of information in this message? Yes, you do. So, I immediately went on Channel 16, "This is Rescue Boat *Phoenix*, Mayday boat fire is in Sheep Pen Cove between Patience and Prudence Islands."

Captain's Log. 06:45 hours August 12. Arriving on scene, I throttled down and could see that the smoke was billowing from a 22-foot inboard/outboard bowrider. The boat was stern anchored to the increasing 15 knot wind and was in a position 200 yards upwind of the anchorage where about 40 boats were moored. Sheep Pen Cove is a favorite overnight destination for local boaters, many of whom were, at this early hour, still below sleeping. I scanned the area and could not see anyone on board or in the water near the burning vessel. As I held position abeam and kept well away from the burning vessel, a quahog fishing boat (commercial clam digger) pulled alongside with two soaking wet passengers, neither of whom was wearing a lifejacket. He said he had just pulled these two young men, let's call them Wet and Wetter, from the water and would I take them aboard the rescue boat so he could go back to working the clam beds? As they boarded my vessel, I handed each of them a lifejacket and my VHF sounded. The Coast Guard wanted to know if I was on scene and they wanted a status report. I asked them to switch and answer Channel 22. Before I could switch my second radio to Channel 22, the Warwick fire boat called on Channel 16, also asking for a situation update. I also asked them to switch and answer Channel 22 so we could get everyone in the loop at the same time.

Getting Seasoned

Captain's Log. 06:50 hours August 12. Before responding, I turned to Wet and Wetter with some questions. "Was there anyone else on board?" No. "How much fuel was on the boat?" About 30 gallons. "Are either of you injured?" No. "How did the fire start?"

Electrical fire in the engine compartment. They saw smoke coming from the engine cover and grabbed a fire extinguisher, which they emptied on the engine and the fire appeared to go out. Then it reignited and flared, evidently igniting a fuel line or fuel leak. They immediately put out a Mayday, and very wisely tossed the anchor into the water, tied it to the starboard stern cleat, and quickly jumped overboard...without lifejackets. The quahogger was nearby, saw them jump into the water, and immediately motored over to fish them out of the water. A true good Samaritan.

Captain's Log. 06:55 hours August 12. As I picked up the radio mic to relay this info, the Warwick fireboat rounded into the channel and headed for the flaming boat, which now had one third of the stern engulfed in flames. The Coast Guard radioed that their responding 34-foot RIB would be on scene in five minutes. The fireboat maneuvered and positioned itself about 40 feet abeam of the burning boat with her bow perpendicular to the wind and facing the flames, and they turned on the forward water cannon. In the meantime, the fireboat had drifted downwind such that the water was not effective as it struck the boat just forward of where the fire was. The fireboat captain repositioned his boat and we could see that the anchor line was now burning down toward the waterline. Just as the water stream hit the fire, the anchor line parted and the boat sank like a stone, sizzling in the water as it went down and extinguishing the fire. I think the boat sinking as the anchor line parted was sheer coincidence. Under normal circumstances a stern anchor would hold the stern down, not up.

Epilogue. Fire on Board #1. Wet and Wetter had lost their boat but other than being rattled and wet, they were none the worse for wear. I thanked them for having the presence of mind to toss an anchor as they dove overboard. Had they not done so, the floating fire could easily have drifted into the anchorage and set one or more additional boats on fire,

146

with who knows what consequences. The local harbormaster and the Coast Guard arrived on scene shortly after the fireboat. The harbormaster took Wet and Wetter on board his boat and returned them safely to shore. The harbormaster contacted Save the Bay to recover the burned-out and sunk boat with their ex-US Navy Mike boat (landing craft with bow ramp). The fireboat and Coast Guard vessel returned to their regular duties and I headed back to base in search of the coffee I had left behind. This entire event took place in less than 30 minutes, and where a fire is involved that is a long time.

By contrast, while working in Honolulu a number of years ago I watched as a 40-foot sailboat's cabin caught fire. I was on a tenth-floor balcony of the Sheraton Waikiki at the time. The boat was anchored less than a mile off Waikiki Beach when I first saw smoke coming from the companionway.

I glanced at my watch and less than one minute later a man and woman came up from below, dived overboard, and swam vigorously away from the boat. At two minutes of elapsed time flames were burning through the boat's catwalks and the mast leaned and fell off the portside. At three minutes elapsed time the boat had literally burned to the waterline and was a smoldering hulk when a rescue boat arrived seven minutes later. Surprisingly, it did not sink. The next day's newspaper said curtains above the alcohol stove had caught fire while the crew was cooking and spread quickly throughout the cabin. This beautiful boat was completely destroyed in just a few minutes.

Captain's Log. Fire on Board #2. 14:00 hours 15 August. It was a sultry late summer afternoon and I was headed north up Narragansett Bay returning from an offshore run, having just disentangled a 36-foot Catalina sailboat from a nearby fish trap. I was running Rescue Boat Three, the 23-foot Steiger, when I spotted a commotion under the Jamestown Bridge. Something didn't look right. A jet ski had moved at high speed up to a 25-foot Regal boat that was anchored next to a bridge py-lon and was hurriedly helping a man, let's call him Lester, off the boat and onto the jet ski. Lester was not wearing a lifejacket. Then I saw the reason for the rapid exit. Dark gray smoke was starting to pour up out of the Regal's cockpit. Even though no Mayday or emergency call had been made I flipped on Rescue Three's strobe lights, added power, and moved to intercept the jet ski that was now running in my direction. Lester yelled out and asked if I could save his boat. Normally in this situation I would have taken Lester aboard, but I felt it would be safer for him to stay on the jet ski since I was approaching a burning vessel.

Neither Lester nor the jet ski operator had a VHF radio or a cell-phone, so we were unable to communicate until we got close enough to shout to each other. A quick situation assessment told me the on-fire boat was anchored, seas were calm at one to two feet, winds brisk at 10-15, and no other boats were in the immediate area. The choices I had were to radio for help and most likely watch the boat burn and sink, or move quickly alongside, board the boat, and try to put the fire out with one of Rescue Boat Three's fire extinguishers before the boat became engulfed in flames. I made a tough choice and came alongside the burning boat and took a double, non-half-hitch turn around its center cleat and board-ed. Blue gray smoke was seeping out from under the inboard/outboard engine's cover. With the cover in place there was no way to hit the base of the fire with the extinguisher. If I lifted the hatch up and it was a fuel fire, there could be a rapid flare up, or maybe even an explosion. I could face serious injury if either happened. If it was an electrical fire, there was a good chance I could put it out with the extinguisher. I lifted the hatch slowly at first, then rapidly when I could see it was an electrical fire. It took only about 20 seconds to extinguish the fire. Whew, that day I definitely had more luck than skill!

Epilogue. Fire on Board #2. Lester had remained nearby on the jet ski, which came alongside the rescue boat when they could see that the fire was extinguished. When asked where he wanted his boat towed to, Lester said, "I don't care where you take it, and I will not get back aboard my boat while it is being towed, or any other time." Ordinarily, rescue boat services require the owner or an owner's rep to be aboard while a vessel is being towed. I made an exception for Lester and suggested three local marinas that might be able to repair his boat engine, which had minimal actual damage. Lester made his marina choice, gave me his phone number, and said he would stop by our office the next morning to square up his bill for services rendered.

This situation, because of immediate danger of sinking, would be classified as a salvage recovery and charges would be negotiated between Lester, his hull insurance company, and Rescue Boat. Salvage charges range from $100 per foot of boat length to more, depending upon boat size and circumstances. In most cases insurance companies send a marine surveyor to look at the damaged vessel, then work out a payment amount with the rescue boat company. In Lester's case the charge was determined to be the minimum of $100 per foot or a total of $2,500. Insurance companies understand the dollar value of their insured vessels and tend to be reasonable in negotiating with rescue services companies who save vessels from becoming a total loss.

It was a fortunate coincidence that Rescue Boat Three was in the right place, at exactly the right time, with the right equipment to save Lester's boat. When all was said and done, I towed Lester's boat back to the marina that housed Rescue Boat base and as promised, Lester stopped by the next morning. I don't know if Lester ever did go back on his boat again.

Episode 24

Captain's Log: *Volvos Don't Float*

Captain Hal Records

In Episode 24, "Volvos Don't Float," Captain Hal lightens the mood and relates two stories of unexpected and funny, at least funny if it isn't happening to you, rescue boat operations. Captain Hal is a professor at a local university and over the years did most of his rescue boat work between May and early September, but he did continue to do runs for emergencies and special situations throughout the year when they did not conflict with his teaching responsibilities. These are two such instances. The first story is the title of this episode, "Volvos Don't Float," and the second story is "My Motor Won't Go."

Captain's Log. Volvos Don't Float. October 7, 17:00 hours. I had just arrived home for dinner after a long day of teaching. It was before happy hour and the sun was indeed over the yardarm. It was a nippy crystal clear 38 degrees outside and I was looking forward to a quiet evening at home when the phone rang. It was Keith, boss captain at Rescue Boat asking, could I help them salvage a Volvo that was underwater in the Great Salt Pond in Point Judith? I agreed to meet him there at the launch ramp in an hour, thinking he would pick me up at the dock with a rescue boat and we would attempt to refloat some kind of boat with a Volvo engine, no doubt an inboard/outboard of some sort. How wrong could I be?

Captain's Log. October 7, 18:00 hours. I pulled up to the ramp amid a bustle of activity. There were two fire trucks with their red emergency lights flashing, one police cruiser with flashing blue lights, and at least a dozen cars and pickup trucks parked randomly in the area. What I did not see was a rescue boat, but I did see Captain Keith's Rescue Boat truck with our salvage trailer in tow as he pulled into the melee. Little

Rescue Boat

Bill, our six foot four salvage diver was in the truck cab with him. Early on I learned not to ask too many questions at the beginning of these kind of operations. What needed to be done, and how I would participate, would become evident soon enough. Captain Keith parked and got out of his truck and immediately was talking with two firemen and a policeman.

It seemed a local boatowner, let's call him Surprised, was getting ready to winterize his boat which had recently been hauled and was blocked on poppets in a nearby boat storage lot. Since it was cold, he had parked his nearly new Volvo station wagon nearby and left the vehicle running with the heat on and windows closed. As it turns out, he had parked near the top of the boat ramp that services the marina. As he left the vehicle and went to gather gear from his boat, what he did not do was to be sure the car transmission was fully engaged in Park, nor did he take the time to set the emergency brake, so—you guessed it. The car had a mind if its own and wanted to go for a swim. It rolled down the steep ramp, gaining a little speed as it went, and slid nicely out into the now pitch-dark water. It remained floating and was caught by the incoming tide and was swept neatly into a nearby salt pond. The vehicle was still running with its lights on as Surprised watched it move around the bend by a stretch of finger piers and ultimately disappear from his sight, at which time he called the local emergency services, hence the police and fire presence. This was not the first time an automobile had been unintentionally launched from this ramp, so the fire department knew just what to do and they immediately called Rescue Boat for assistance.

Captain's Log. October 7, 18:30 hours. Surprised's vehicle had first floated into a nearby salt pond on the inbound tide. Then it reversed direction as the tide changed and began to ebb, floating the vehicle out of the salt pond and drifting it back toward the ramp. During this time, the vehicle was taking on more and more water. Although Volvo builds a very tight and high-quality vehicle, they are not built to withstand being launched into the water! At some point while the car was drifting the engine drowned and stopped running, and the car finally sank in about eight feet of water. It came to rest on the mud bottom immediately adjacent to a finger pier, which was very convenient for us. This explains why Captain Keith and Little Bill arrived in a truck and not a rescue boat. The plan was to move our salvage gear onto the pier near the vehicle and raise the car in much the same way as we had done many times with sunken boats.

While Bill donned his wetsuit and dive gear, Keith and I moved scuba tanks, a bank of emergency lights, a gasoline driven air compressor fitted with an output manifold, and three 2,000 pound capacity marine pillow type salvage airbags onto the pier. The plan was for Bill to get into the cold water and use lines to attach one airbag under the front bumper, a second under the rear bumper, and the third in the cabin of the car via the conveniently located sunroof. When the air bags were properly secured to the vehicle, Bill surfaced, and we passed him three air hoses, each containing a special fitting that mated with the airbags. He attached air hoses to each airbag, working from the front of the Volvo to the rear. Since this car obviously had a mind of its own, he attached an especially long and durable red line, which was kindly provided by the fire department, to the running gear under the front fender of the car so that it could not escape again and drift out to sea once it was refloated.

Captain's Log. October 7, 19:30 hours. Unlike some complicated salvage operations that we have performed, all went according to plan. Keith fired up the compressor and in sequence used the output air manifold to begin inflating the front airbag, then the center, and then the rear. Bill was standing on top of the car with water up to his shoulders as the flotation process began.

Slowly but surely Bill began to rise out of the water as though he was a mystical Greek God of the Sea, until the car was floating with him standing triumphantly on top of its roof. About twenty-five onlookers in the parking lot let out a piercing whistle and gave a loud round of applause for Little Bill's efforts and very stylish rise from the sea.

Rescue Boat

Surprised's car was now floating along on three puffy airbags and drifted away from the pier while a group of firemen controlled the long red safety line and fed out enough rope for the car to <u>almost</u> reach the boat ramp, at which point they tossed the bitter end of the rope into the water to Little Bill, who was swimming alongside the car. He then grabbed the line and swam the remaining distance to the ramp. Meanwhile a flatbed wrecker truck summoned by the police had arrived and backed down the ramp to the waterline. Bill attached the hook from the truck's tow cable to the long red rope and the car was pulled slowly to the ramp where it could be properly and securely attached directly to the

truck's tow cable and winched up out of the water and onto the bed of the truck. The tow truck operator was successful in retrieving and loading the vehicle without incident and he secured it to the bed of the truck in preparation for transport to the tow yard.

Epilogue. Volvos Don't Float. This episode speaks to the effective use of air bags for conducting salvage operations. We will revisit this in future episodes, but suffice it to say at this point that the combination of good planning, the mechanical advantage of well-placed strong flotation devices, and good old Yankee ingenuity can move mountains, or at least very large and very sunk or very beached and grounded boats...and cars. Surprised was pleased to get his car back, however, it was declared a total loss by the insurance company. Once salt water encroaches into a vehicle, the electrical components, as well as the mechanical components, will suffer almost immediate corrosion. The sheet metal will rust, and the fabric will disintegrate over time. Because the engine was running before the car went underwater there were opportunities for the salt water to enter the engine itself and cause serious damage.

I am not sure how Rescue Boat charged for that job. For my part, I made sure not to buy any used Volvos for a while. It is also worthwhile to note that a vehicle that has been in a flood has the same opportunity for destructive corrosion and water damage. Being submerged for even a short period of time even in fresh water will cause irreparable damage to a vehicle.

Captain's Log. "My Motor Won't Go". October 12. 14:30 hours. This was the week for unusual calls. First, we were asked to retrieve a sunken Volvo car and now someone was on the phone saying his engine will not go. Let's call him Nogo. Whenever possible we try to diagnose and sometimes even resolve boater problems without dispatching a rescue boat. This saves us time, saves the customer money, and builds goodwill.

I asked Nogo, "Will your motor run at all?"

He said, "Yes, it starts and runs fine."

I asked Nogo, "Does the throttle work, and can you control the speed of the motor?"

He said, "Yes, no problem."

I asked, "Can you shift the engine?"

Again, he said, "Yes, it just wouldn't go."

I asked for his location, and he replied that he was safely anchored about one half mile from the launch ramp at Bold Point in Providence, and had just stopped and put the motor in reverse to pick up a hat that had flown away from his girlfriend as the boat gained speed. He gave me his lat/long after which I grabbed my go bag, boarded Rescue Boat *Osprey* (a 26-foot Cat with a pair of 175 Suzuki outboards) and headed for his location.

Captain's Log. October 12. 15:15 hours. Arriving on scene I tied up alongside Nogo's boat, asked him to start the engine, and listened as he went through the drill of advancing the throttle and shifting, while all the time watching to see if any flashing error code signals appeared on his engine control screen. All seemed well so I asked him what and

154

when was the most recent service to his engine. Nogo said that yesterday he had pulled his propeller to grease the shaft. Bingo!! We likely had a propeller problem, so I asked Nogo to raise his outdrive to its highest position. We both stared over the transom as the outdrive lifted out of the water and we saw that the outdrive had no propeller......which pretty much explained why his boat would not go.

Epilogue. My Boat Won't Go. Evidently Nogo had neglected to replace the cotter pin that secures the propeller nut, and hence the propeller to the splined propeller shaft, but he had tightened the nut just enough to hold the prop in place while he backed off the dock at the launch ramp. However, after taking the boat away from the ramp at a moderate speed, he stopped and put the boat in reverse to retrieve the wind-blown hat, the nut loosened and came off, and the propeller spun off the shaft when he put the boat into gear. Nogo did not have a spare propeller so I towed him back to the launch ramp and he called it a day. I returned to base, still smiling.

A message for all mariners: If you are not sure of proper procedures, it is best to have a professional perform maintenance on your boat's propulsion system. In Nogo's case, a simple ten cent cotter pin left off during the final prop assembly cost him the price of a new prop plus a service call from the rescue boat. Also, if he cannot find the missing cotter pin, he would be out an additional ten cents to purchase a new one! As a further note of caution, it is not uncommon for propellers containing an internal rubber hub to "spin" that hub under excessive load. When this happens, the boat's behavior is exactly the same as if there were no propeller at all. The most common cause of spinning a hub is towing, or attempting to tow, something too large for your boat. I have done this myself trying to be a good Samaritan and tow a 34-foot powerboat with my 21-foot personal boat. About halfway back to the harbor my boat kept running but stopped moving. The propeller was there but no longer turning because the rubber hub had spun out. It is great to help someone out, just be sure the effort doesn't result in two vessels being towed instead of one.

Episode 25

Captain's Log: *Daredevils*

Captain Robert Behling

In Episode 25 Captain Bob begins his adventures near the Hudson River in New York, takes us back to Cape Cod, and then on to the Outer Banks of North Carolina. He turns back the hands of time to his younger days and provides a glimpse into the kinds of adventures that teach a love of the water and ultimately cause people to become mariners. The kind of mariners that may join the military, become professional boatmen and captains, or just plain enjoy mucking around on boats and on the water like most of us do. So, if you want to be, or perhaps already are, a daredevil, check out these four stories, very cleverly named Daredevil #1 to #4, each of which has its own epilogue. These stories can be particularly poignant and please be aware that we do not suggest that anyone try anything like this.

Captain's Log: Daredevil #1. The best fishing spots are often the hardest to get to. I grew up in southern New York State, where the Croton River meets the Hudson River. The Hudson was our connection with salt water, and seasonal fish and crabs came up the Hudson. There was also a resident population of fish that we tried to catch all year. When you are a kid without a boat, finding a good spot to wet a line was a challenge. A friend and I managed to stumble upon a rocky point that was almost inaccessible but usually held fish. The chal-

156

lenge was getting to our spot; the only way was to cross a railroad trestle that spanned a wide river inlet. No problem, we were self-confident kids and we could do it!

We fished the spot and usually had good luck, so we kept going back. One bright and clear afternoon in the middle of the summer the fishing urge hit us, so we grabbed a can of worms and our gear and headed for our spot. As we were crossing the trestle there was a loud rumbling, and we turned and saw a freight train bearing down on us. There was not enough time for us to get off the bridge, so we had a moment of panic. It was a one-track structure with little room to spare between the track and the guardrails. Our decision was to back up against the guard railing, suck in our stomach and hang on, and stay as still as possible while the train went by. I am able to tell this story, so I guess our strategy was successful!

Epilogue. I am not sure if the train engineer even saw us, I do remember the train did not slow down as it crossed the trestle. Then again, a long freight train takes miles to slow momentum, which would be too late to keep us from getting hurt if our strategy did not work. I remember feeling the pressure bubble in front of the engine, then it was a blast of wind as the cars zoomed by us at what we thought was a very high rate of speed. Eventually the caboose came into view, then it was gone, and we were safe! Who knows, maybe we were like Washington Irving's *Legend of Sleepy Hollow*, which was also situated near the Hudson River, and were destined to continue forth as was the Headless Horseman in that story. As they say, strange things sometimes happen, and as it turns out my dad built a new home on Sleepy Hollow Road the summer before I left for college. In any event, that day we decided it made good sense to hunt for another secret fishing spot that did not require crossing a railroad trestle to access it.

Where I lived the railroad tracks ran along the Hudson River, usually right on the banks, so if you wanted river access to fish you had to deal with crossing the tracks. Because there were regulations requiring train propulsion to be electric only from our town into New York City, we always had to be cognizant of the energized rail providing the engine with electric power that ran about a foot above ground level parallel with the tracks. One misstep when crossing the track and bumping into the third rail could cause you to become a "crispy critter" in a flash! That made a lasting impression on all the kids that hung around the river and regularly crossed the tracks. Obviously, I survived these hazards and moved on to fishing mountain streams and lakes, along with salt water, during my college years and beyond. I do not remember ever trying to cross the tracks again after I graduated from high school.

Captain's Log. Daredevil #2. Teens acting stupid in a speedboat. One of my childhood fishing friends lived on the river and had a small dock for his speedboat and canoe. We all envied him; he could boat and fish whenever he wanted. He had ordered a build-it-yourself speedboat kit and he and his father put it together and installed a Mercury 20 horsepower, which in its day was a good-sized outboard engine and it was equipped with Quicksilver drive. My memory of this is faint aside from it was supposed to double the prop revolutions to increase the speed of a small and light boat. In any event, the boat was small and light, could only hold two people and went like the wind. My friend, call him David, asked me if I wanted to go out on the Hudson and have some fun with the tourists. I decided to join him on the water for whatever he wanted to do, so off we went.

There were, plying the waters in and around New York City, large tourist sightseeing boats we called Day-liners. They were comfortable but slow: the perfect target for our pranks. David would stand off about 100 yards, set a course for the bow of the Day-liner, and give the speedboat full throttle. It would jump up into a plane, and before you knew it, we were on a collision course! At the last minute he would spin the wheel and skid past the bow of the Day-liner, circle around, and do the same thing on the other side! A twelve-foot boat challenging one over one hundred feet is no contest, but we did create some startled looks on the faces of the passengers. At our level of immaturity, we thought we were having fun. The captain of the Day-liner was probably tearing his hair out in frustration! It was only good luck that there was no Coast Guard intervention during these pranks, although I am sure we could outrun any cutter they might send, and that we could always duck into shallow water where larger Coast Guard vessels could not follow.

Rescue Boat

Epilogue. At the time we were pulling these pranks I did not know much about power boats. I did not know that steering cables can become corroded and weak, often breaking under severe stress. I did not know that judging speed on the water is different from judging speed on land (my extensive experience was limited to a bicycle) where there is no tide or wave action. David knew more about these things than I did but he liked living life on the edge. He liked to push the envelope, for example during our high school basketball days, he was my teammate with the most floor burns from making drives and dives that put him on the floor more times than not. We headed in different directions for college, were busy with summer jobs and drifted apart as we grew out of our teen years. Unfortunately, shortly after graduating from college, David was negotiating a mountain road at night, late to get home so he was pushing it a little, and he hit another vehicle head on. He was not wearing a seatbelt and his impact with the steering wheel exploded his heart and he died instantly.

Captain's Log. Daredevil #3. A hole in one. You might be wondering why golf shows up in stories about the sea. Well, I stole the comment from golfing, and applied it to fishing. Once again, I return to Cape Cod, this time as a summer visitor from my home in Idaho. My children were growing up very quickly, and I wanted them to experience some of the wonder of the Cape that I encountered as a child: digging clams, fishing off the jetty, looking for blackberries, catching crabs in the backwaters, and attending Friday night band concerts in the town park.

When we vacationed on the Cape, we would often take walks exploring the backroads, woods, and hidden beaches. On one delightful summer day I took my oldest son on a walk to a small beach on a nearby salt pond where four or five commercial shellfish fishermen searched for clams and moored their boats. Everybody likes to go to a beach where there are boats, there is always so much to see and experience. When we arrived at the beach, we encountered one of the commercial fishermen trying to get his sunk 16-foot wooden boat off the bottom and up onto the beach. We gave him a hand and I noticed the boat had several round holes in the bottom. Very strange!

Getting Seasoned

As we assisted in retrieving the boat I commented on the round holes, and the fisherman, we can call him Tom, started telling us a story. He fished the pond, mainly "scratching" for quahogs, a hard-shell clam prized for both chowder for the large ones and eating raw for the small ones, called "little necks." He harvested the clams using a "bull rake," which is a rake much like a garden rake with a basket attached behind the teeth and a long handle. You drop the head of the rake to the bottom, drag it over the sand and scratch up a clam, which then rolls into the basket. When you have captured a basketful you lift the rake out of the water and remove the clams. That week Tom was having a challenging time finding a productive clam bed, and did not pay attention to where he was fishing as he prospected the salt pond for quahogs. He finally found a good spot and harvested a large basket of clams, but in doing so he did not realize that he had encroached on beds claimed by one of the other fishermen. The fishermen had agreed to abide by an unwritten rule about where they could search and harvest clams, and he had crossed the line into another fisherman's territory. He was spotted and reported. The offended fisherman was responsible for assessing penalties, and his penalty was to go to the mooring that night, drill several holes in the bottom of Tom's boat, and watch it slowly sink to the bottom. Cape Cod Justice. No physical violence. No arguing. No vendetta. Just a clear message: Keep away from my space and clams!

The most interesting thing was that Tom knew he was in the wrong and was not mad at or seeking revenge against the hole-drilling fisherman. In fact, he told me that he deserved it, and was glad that the punishment was not worse! This is a great lesson for all and should be extended as well to messing with someone else's lobster or crab pots or fish traps. Just don't do it. It isn't right and as in this story it can have disastrous results.

Epilogue. The important lesson here is to know the local rules, and do not challenge or create a conflict with someone unless you are willing to suffer the consequences. When you moor a boat, it is exposed to the public and anything can and might happen given the right set of circumstances. During the ensuing years I occasionally encountered Tom fishing in the pond, apparently at peace with the others who fished the area as well. Then one winter there was a strong storm, and the access from the pond to the bay, and the bay to the ocean, was changed by drifting sands. The new access allowed whelk (snails) to enter the pond, and their main diet is juvenile clams. Within a year the pond was almost devoid of quahogs, and the fishermen moved on. I took it upon myself to catch some whelk (easy to rake up with a clam rake) and grind them up for chowder. I had visited St. Thomas and had some conch chowder, which was quite good. Unfortunately, whelk are nowhere near as tasty as Caribbean conch or Cape quahogs, so I had to find a new place to dig for clams.

Captain's Log. Daredevil #4. Keep your eye on the water. In this story we move to the Outer Banks of North Carolina, where I had just completed building a house in anticipation of retirement. I built in a large community with mixed housing including condos, townhouses, and private homes, with both bay and ocean access. We had a nice marina near my new house, and I enjoyed hanging around and seeing what the catch of the day was. I had a 14-foot skiff at the time that I kept at home and trailered it to the launch ramp at the marina.

While hanging around the marina I became acquainted with Don and Nancy, a couple who recently retired and moved to the area from Long Island. Nancy's father Chuck lived in our development in one of the waterfront condos adjacent to the marina, and they spent a lot of time with him working on updating his boat. Chuck was from New Jersey and had scaled down from a 50-foot Egg Harbor cruiser to a 25-foot Wellcraft fisherman when he moved to North Carolina, and he was trying to fit it out like his bigger boat so he could take it safely offshore. His latest addition was an autopilot that had just been installed. Chuck decided to take a cruise and test it out.

Chuck had a somewhat hyper personality, and he was always trying to do two things at once. He started up and took the Wellcraft out of the marina, through the channel to the bay, lined up with the outbound marker buoys, and pushed the throttles on the twin outboards to turn 3,600 RPM. He enjoyed going fast! As he rounded the first buoy, he engaged the autopilot for a two mile straight run to the ocean entrance. Wait a minute…the Wellcraft was not properly responding and holding course! It was wavering and coming off point regularly. Something was wrong; either the mechanic hooked the equipment up incorrectly or there was a short, blown fuse or something interrupting the rudder signal and the navigation gear.

The readout came to the helm, but most of the equipment was installed in the cabin, so Chuck opened the cabin hatch and went for a look. As he was scouting around trying to identify the problem, he heard a loud crash and felt the boat bounce around. He immediately climbed back to the helm to see what had happened. Bobbing in the middle of the channel was the remains of a 17-foot canoe and two people hanging on for dear life to their life vests. He had forgotten to disengage the autopilot, retard the throttles, and put the engines in neutral before climbing into the cabin. In fact, he did not even look around checking to see if there were any obstacles in his path or in the area. He hit the canoe going about 25 knots

per hour, cleanly broke it in half, and put the occupants into the bay. Fortunately, there were no injuries.

Epilogue. Captain Hal often talks about situational awareness and being cognizant of what is going on around you. This is a case where Captain Chuck neglected basic safety principles. He should have disengaged his engines and scanned his surroundings before leaving the bridge. Instead, he focused on his electronic issues only, and lost track of where his craft was going or what was in front of him. In talking with his daughter Nancy after the accident, she told me he was quick to see the error of his ways and offered immediate restitution to the soaked canoeists. Nancy also told me that Don lectured Chuck about not taking the boat out alone and told him to call if he wanted to go boating and he would come over and go with him. A second pair of eyes is always a good thing when on the water and situational awareness is an absolute must if you are to remain safe.

Captain's Comment. Autopilot systems can be inherently dangerous and require special attention from any person using them. While on duty at Rescue Boat, Captain Hal received an emergency call from the captain of a 42-foot yacht, let's call him Dangerous, returning to Cuttyhunk, Massachusetts from south of Montauk, New York. He had set his autopilot for the #1 Block Island buoy, went below, and fell asleep. After being underway for some time Dangerous awoke to a terrible crash as his boat lurched to port. He had hit the buoy squarely on his starboard bow and at first thought he was sinking. As it turns out he had torn a hole in the bow about three feet above the waterline and was able to make it to a nearby marina.

In another very sad instance, a rescue boat was called by the Coast Guard to a nearshore accident where a 45-foot boat operating on autopilot with the captain and a crewmember below hit a small boat and instantly killed its occupant, who was fishing in open water. The boat was treated as a crime scene and Rescue Boat towed it to a nearby marina where it was immediately hauled and impounded by the authorities. The collision impact was so severe that parts of the small boat were found wedged between the prop shafts and prop struts of the larger boat.

I do not know how the legal actions in this case were resolved, but one thing is for sure: While on the water, persons using autopilot and all others in the vicinity of where they are being used must be on constant vigil. You never know whether a boat on an apparent collision course with you has anyone on its bridge or not. In order to remain safe, you can try to call the vessel on Channel 16 and/or take evasive action immediately. Just as with automobiles, defensive driving is the smart thing to do when you are on the water, especially because boats on autopilot can be more like unguided missiles than vessels under human control.

Episode 26

Captain's Log: *Marine Salvage Challenges*

Captain Hal Records

Salvage is a scary idea to many boaters and there are many misconceptions about what it really is and how salvage is done. In Episode 26, "Marine Salvage Challenges," Captain Hal relates the dynamics of three rescue boat salvage operations. These stories are: #1 "Rocks Make Holes in Boats," #2 "Beached," and #3 "My Boat Sank."

Captain's Log: #1 Rocks Make Holes in Boats. Hurricane Bob (no relation to Captain Bob) had just blown through New England in early September and left in its wake a lot of beached, sunk, and wrecked boats. There were so many wrecks scattered over the bays and beaches that it was necessary for Rescue Boat to triage a number of these to create a logical and productive salvage plan. There were boats blown aground onto the rocks and lifted well above the normal high tide waterline that were so severely damaged they needed to be extracted with a chainsaw and crane or front end loader. A once stately Sea Ray cruiser was pushed by the storm high and dry on a roadbed about 20 feet above sea level. The port side of her hull was ripped from the gunnel, her propellers and shafts were gone, and there was not enough bottom left to repair.

There were also many boats that had been blown onto the rocks that could be salvaged us-
ing airbags, and techniques like those described in Episode 24, "Volvos Don't Float," and there were many boats that needed hull repair before salvage bags could be used to re-

cover them. The Catalina sailboat here illustrates severe damage requiring temporary repairs before salvage operations could begin. After the storm, rescue boat companies, shipyards with floating cranes, and salvage divers were kept busy with the high volume of salvaged vessels that needed to be retrieved and taken out of the water for inspection, repair, or scrapping. Our first salvage operation from that storm was a severely damaged and beached sailboat.

The boat had broken loose from her mooring across the harbor and the stormy sea smashed her onto a rocky shore and wedged the craft into the rocks. The prop was gone, the strut was bent, and the cutlass bearing broken. There were holes in the starboard side that I could walk through, and the keel had been gouged. Other than that, and of course a broken rudder, drowned engine, and drenched interior soaked in diesel fuel, she was in fairly good condition!

The salvage process was to first unceremoniously screw a 4x8 sheet of quarter-inch plywood over each of the holes in her hull. Screws were placed about two inches apart along the edges. The second step was to cover the plywood snugly with blue tarps drawn tight by ropes wrapped around the entire boat. The third step was to duct tape the ropes to the tarps and the tarps to the hull so they would not shift while the boat was being towed. The fourth step was to attach and inflate airbags in the same manner as described in *Episode 24 "Volvos Don't Float"*. The fifth and riskiest step was to wait for high tide and then use a rescue boat to skid the boat off the rocky beach—without ripping off the airbags or our "finely crafted" hull patches.

Epilogue. #1 Rocks Make Holes in Boats. The sailboat was successfully extracted from the rocky beach and survived a 60-minute tow to a nearby marina, where it was hauled immediately upon arrival. The sailboat was subsequently declared a total loss by the insurance company and was scrapped. The scrap process for boats is to remove anything metal, including engines, lifeline posts, masts, keel, and any other metal scrap items. Then, a chainsaw is used to cut the hull into manageable sized pieces which are loaded onto a dump truck for transfer to a disposal site. Goodbye faithful sailboat.

Getting Seasoned

One good thing that resulted from Hurricane Bob was that the town promulgated a whole new mooring procedure requiring boat and mooring owners to have adequate ground tackle for the size and weight of their boats, and to have their moorings inspected at least once every three years. Since the storm, the local harbormaster has faithfully enforced these requirements, and although there have been a few breakaways during storms, there has never since been a repeat of the wreckage caused by Hurricane Bob.

Captain's Log: #2 Beached. July 28. 10:00 hours. Salvages take many forms, and as described in previous episodes, Rescue Boat's priority is to try and prevent occurrences that might result in a salvage. It was a sunny late July morning. I was operating Rescue Boat *Phoenix*, the 26-foot RIB, and was just completing a jumpstart in Newport Harbor when Dispatch called my cell with what should have been an easy run. The weather was good, the wind was southwest and in my favorite velocity range of about five knots, and my fuel tanks were full, but my little voice was speaking, *"Beware the day."* The vessel needing assistance was fishing offshore, and according to the information from dispatch it was a 28-foot Bayliner. The boat's captain, let's call him Adrift, had lost power and was drifting toward Third Beach in Newport. This is an ocean facing beach about 45 minutes from my current location. Dispatch had given me his lat/long, which when plugged into my GPS showed him to be uncomfortably close to the beach.

Captain's Log: July 28. 10:15 hours. Upon completing the jumpstart, I headed *Phoenix* south around Castle Hill and toward the mouth of the bay and added power as I encountered a gentle three-foot ground swell. As is normal procedure I called Adrift's cellphone to see how he was doing, asked for his current lat/long, and gave him my estimated ETA at his location. Because his location appeared to be awfully close to the beach, I asked Adrift if he had anchored, to which he said no.

I asked if he had enough anchor line to anchor where he was and he responded, "Yes, and I will anchor now." Ok, good…. but *my little voice* was still saying *"Beware."*

Rescue Boat

Captain's Log: July 28. 10:45 hours. When I arrived on scene about a mile south of Newport, there was no sign of Adrift's boat. I scanned the horizon seaward and then peered in the direction of the beach, where I could see a boat which appeared to be on the beach. Sure enough, it was Adrift. He was not really adrift at all. He was firmly planted on the beach with his beam to the gently rolling three-foot swell which lifted and then set the boat back down with each successive wave. Approaching the beach, I tilted *Phoenix's* 175 hp Suzuki outboards as high out of the water as they would go and still keep their water pumps and telltales pumping. I approached to within about 50 yards of the beach where I was rapidly running out of water depth. From there Adrift hailed me to say that his anchor did not hold. I could in fact see that his anchor was in two feet of water about halfway between my bow and his boat. Evidently, he had not deployed his anchor until his boat was bouncing off the hard pack sand bottom. *Hello little voice.*

Adrift had fortunately tilted the outdrive of his single Mercruiser up such that it was not digging into the sand. This was beginning to look a lot like a salvage operation, but because he was a member, Rescue Boat's membership agreement states that there would be no charge if Adrift's boat could be refloated by one rescue boat in 15 minutes of time. As it turns out the tide was coming in, the Bayliner was being moved by the waves, and hence there was a chance that he could be pulled off the beach quickly.

Under the circumstances and because of the water depth, I could not swing my stern to face the beach, so I kept my stern to the sea and spooled off about 75 yards of hawser which I carried to the bow. From there I was able to throw the heavy stainless snap attached to the end of the line to Adrift, who was now standing in waist deep water between *Phoenix* and his boat. He pulled the line towards the beach and attached the snap to the bow ring of his boat. Ordinarily, we would have deployed a bridle at the end of the hawser and attached it to his bow cleats, but in this case that would result in a downward pull that would drive his boat down and further into the sand, making it more difficult to move. By using the bow eye, the pull would be in a generally upward direction, and hence reducing the drag of the hull on the sand. Once the hawser was attached to the Bayliner, I asked Adrift and his two passengers to stay out of the boat and if possible, push on the hull when appropriate. They would have the opportunity to get back aboard via the swim platform once the boat was floated, or at least nearly floated. Getting passengers off beached vessels makes them lighter, in this case by about 500 pounds, and hence easier to tow while beached."

Captain's Log: July 28. 11:30 hours. Once everyone was in position and ready, I backed *Phoenix* into the sea while gradually feeding out nearly all 200 yards of one-inch woven poly hawser, at which point I rotated *Phoenix's* bow to the sea. Long hawsers stretch and any line, no matter how strong, under enough pressure will snap. When the line snaps and flails around, there is always the possibility of decapitating or seriously injuring anyone nearby. That is why many, if not most, rescue boats have metal cages located between the boat operator and the tow post to which the hawser is attached. In this operation once the tow hawser was drawn tight, I kept easy pressure on the throttles and as a wave lifted the boat up off the beach, I applied power. On the first pull the bow of Adrift's boat turned about three feet toward the sea. On the second another three feet, and so on until her bow was pointing directly to sea and directly toward my stern. From there the three-foot waves were just big enough to lift the boat so that in a sequence of about six waves *Phoenix* was able to pull her seaward into deep enough water to float.

Epilogue. #2 Beached. In many cases, salvage operations are all about geometry. There are times that power does give an advantage, but repositioning the hull, matching the application of power to the height and timing of the waves, and not trying to accomplish the whole operation in one pull generally works out better than a very aggressive "go for broke" approach. In this case, I took the time to take it slow and move the Bayliner in small increments. Once his boat was floating, Adrift and his crew climbed back aboard and the tow back to his home port, although about four hours long, was uneventful. There was no charge for the ungrounding and Adrift was a very pleased and grateful Rescue Boat member. It is common while staffing the Rescue Boat booth at boat shows in the dead of winter to have happy customers, including Adrift, stop by to say hello and again express their appreciation. For me, this is one of the more rewarding perks of being a rescue boat captain.

Captain's Note. A behavior not commonly encountered by everyday boaters is that a boat, including towboats and even those having twin engines, when attached by the stern to an immovable object such as a boat on the beach, will pull in a straight line only up to a point. Adding power causes the towing vessel to skate rapidly to starboard and then rapidly to port at ever increasing speeds until all traction is lost and power is reduced. It feels like the boat is on ice and she becomes nearly impossible to control. I have experienced this in the dead of winter when two rescue boats were used while attempting to pull a 44-foot, heavy, deep keeled sailboat off a beach. The tow boats' hawsers were both attached to the bow of the beached boat and power applied until both towboats skated from side to side, bumping into each other in the middle. The lesson learned was to use either a big commercial tugboat in the water or a large crawler tractor on the beach to move such obstinate objects. That turned out to be one of the very few attempted salvages that we were not able to do. In the end, the boat owner hired a local construction crew that, with special permission, brought heavy equipment to the beach and literally dug a canal to float the boat off the beach at high tide.

Captain's Log: #3 My Boat Sank. Boats sinking at moorings are a common occurrence, most frequently caused by bilge pumps failing; the batteries powering the bilge pumps becoming dead from old age; continued use during long or multiple storms; outboard boats with low cut transoms shipping water over the transom in a storm; and/or boats being pulled under due to short or fouled mooring chains and painters in a storm surge. This story tells the tale of just such a sinking.

Captain's Log: August 12. 11:30 hours. It was Monday and Rescue Boat had a very busy weekend servicing numerous calls for assistance. Late Sunday evening a series of severe thunderstorms rolled through the region, spawning microbursts in a few locations around the bay. This morning we began to receive calls from boat owners who had discovered their boats had sunk at their moorings overnight in the microbursts. As with the hurricane described in #1 "Rocks Make Holes in Boats," we first triaged three sunken boats and developed a plan to salvage each one. Unlike the previous situation where most of the salvage work took place on a rocky beach, these sunken boats were all in the water and still attached to their mooring painters. Hence the salvage operations would be done with a rescue boat.

In preparation for the first salvage, a 28-foot cabin cruiser, we loaded air bags, a gasoline powered air compressor, an air distribution manifold, several lines, one gasoline powered and two electric dewatering pumps along with two scuba tanks and other assorted diving gear into Rescue Boat *Valiant*, a 26-foot Pro Cat Catamaran with a pair of 175 horsepower Suzuki outboards. A catamaran hull is particularly well suited for salvage work. They are very stable, highly maneuverable, have good deck space, and most importantly have large and stable swim ladders mounted between the twin hulls and engines, which make them diver friendly. When "Little Bill" our six foot four diver arrived, we headed out to Mount Hope Bay for the first salvage operation.

Captain's Log: August 12. 12:30 hours. Arriving on scene we found the sunken vessel, let's call her *Downunder*, sitting on the bottom still attached to her mooring painter. We pulled alongside and Little Bill eased himself into the water to take a look at *Downunder's* condition, paying special attention to any hull damage or possible leaks. Fortunately, there did not appear to be any damage that would prevent her from floating with the assistance of airbags.

The next phase of the salvage operation was to secure two 4,000-pound lift capacity airbags under the stern, and two 2,000 lift capacity airbags under the bow. The lift was done in much the same manner as was done with the Volvo in Episode 24, by partially inflating one airbag at a time in rotation to keep *Downunder* rising evenly in the water column. There is the possibility of the boat being lifted turning turtle and rolling over, which is always a concern.

Captain's Log: August 12. 13:30 hours. As *Downunder* gradually arose from the depths we could see some minor damage done to her canopy top and isinglass enclosures and windshield.

Sunk boats are buffeted by waves in a storm, even while underwater, and can be banged and rubbed against the bottom. The goal of the lifting process was to get *Downunder's* gunnels above the water level, if possible six inches or more, and then to pass dewatering pumps from the rescue boat into the boat being raised.

As *Downunder* gained buoyancy and height above the surface of the water, she was tied alongside Rescue Boat *Valiant* until she was pumped nearly dry. In this case she was not taking on water, so the pumps were turned off, but left aboard in case she sprung a leak while

being towed to the Swansea launch ramp. We also left the airbags in place... just in case. We took Big Bill's tank and fins aboard *Valiant* and he climbed up the stern ladder to dry off.

Oddly enough, and I am not sure why it is so, but sunken center console powerboats with T-tops tend to turn turtle while being recovered more often than other boats. I have seen them do this when being raised by airbags, and even when being raised from the bottom by a crane on a barge using straps.

Epilogue. #3 My Boat Sank. *Downunder* was slowly and successfully towed to a nearby launch ramp where a local marina awaited with a truck and trailer and hauled the boat. The forward airbags were removed before Rescue Boat *Valiant* carefully guided and slid *Downunder* onto the trailer. The aft airbags were removed after hauling and can be seen stretched out on the ramp. *Downunder* was not declared a total loss by the insurance company, but clearly needed some TLC and most likely a new engine before returning to sea.

Captain's Note. Marine salvage jobs are not for the faint of heart. The process of salvaging sunken or damaged vessels is dangerous work. It is distressing for those who love boats to see them so severely damaged, and raising them requires much skill, patience, and specialized equipment. Every salvage is different, and some of the more challenging salvage operations occur in winter, occasionally through the ice. Here again, as Captain Keith says, being a rescue boat captain is not for everyone.

Episode 27
Captain's Log: *So Who Needs Steering?*
Captain Robert Behling and Captain Hal Records

In this episode, "So Who Needs Steering," we focus on boat steering issues. Sadly, losing steering on the water is more common than might be expected, so in the interest of safety this episode relates two tales of what can happen when the steering on a boat fails. The first is about a spring striped bass fishing trip with Bob's son, who had come to Cape Cod to join him for a weekend of fishing. The second is a rescue boat story of steering failure on a high-performance boat.

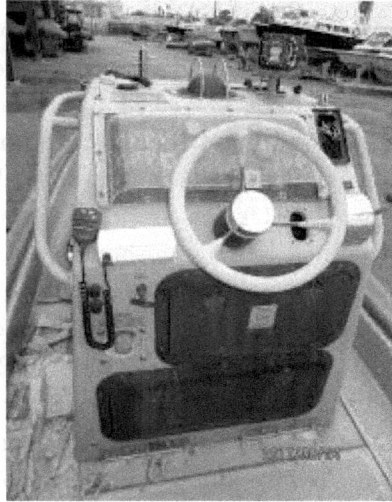

Prologue. Both Captain Hal and I spend most of our time during the fall, winter, and spring in the university classroom. When summer comes, Captain Hal puts his boat handling skills to work with rescuing mariners in distress. I stay closer to home with family responsibilities taking up much of my time. However, when the forsythia begins to bloom and the striped bass arrive, you will usually find me in my boat and wetting a line. My three grown children enjoy fishing as much as I do, and willingly join me on the water whenever they can.

#1. No Fish Today. Fishing the waters around Cape Cod during the winter months generally involves a nice (or perhaps chilly) boat ride and hamburgers for dinner. The fin fish abandon the inshore cold waters of the Cape, coming back in the spring when things warm up. There is

173

always shell fishing in the winter, which I do with regularity, and which does not require the use of a boat. The clam flats and oyster beds are accessible by vehicle and on foot, with nothing more than a pair of insulated waders needed to get you where the shellfish live. So, after winterizing, my boat sits idle for several months until the water warms and the fish return. This weekend would be the first outing of the spring, and we were both looking forward to some time on the water and grilled striped bass for dinner.

A brief check finds everything in order on my boat, a full tank of gas, a charged battery and appropriate tackle on board. The trailer tires are fully inflated and ready to roll. We hook up the boat trailer to my pickup truck and head for a launch ramp, which is located about five miles from my house on a harbor accessing Nantucket Sound. The boat slides off the rails in the water, the motor starts right up, and after parking the truck and trailer we head out to open water. It is a delightful morning, lots of sunshine, and the air is rapidly warming up. We soon shed our jackets as we make our way to Monomoy Point, where I heard there were some nice bass being caught. Seas are calm, and we make our way under full power for about 20 minutes before we see the turbulence created by a sandbar and tidal movement. The "suds" and front line of the turbulence are our target for the day's fishing, and the excitement builds as we join several other boats working the waters.

Captain's Log: Getting on the Fish. There is a pretty strong tide running over the bar creating a lot of pull on the boat, and I find that I need to continually maneuver and position the boat to give my son the best opportunity to present his lure in just the right spot. We have fished this area for years and have a good feel for where we would find the bass. He barely gets a line wet when disaster strikes! My steering cable breaks, and I cannot turn the motor to control the motion and direction of the boat. I carry tools and spare parts on board, but not something as large as a steering cable. Besides, this is not something you want to try and change while at sea. So, fishing is put on hold and boat management takes residence. We know we need to return to port, and we know that we need some degree of steering to accomplish that.

Rescue Boat

Captain's Log: Mechanical Malfunction. We work out a plan: my son will sit on the transom and manually turn and adjust the motor to provide steering. I will keep our speed down so he can hold on to the motor without risking falling overboard, and what is usually less than a half hour run becomes two hours to return to the boat ramp and get the boat back on the trailer. We made the trip without incident, but I often think about what would have happened if I were alone on this fishing trip to Monomoy, which I often was over the years. It would have been much harder to control the boat and make it back to the safety of the port. At this time there was no rescue boat service available for these waters.

After returning home I parked and unhitched the boat. We decided that a pot of clam chowder would be a good substitute for grilled fish, so we threw rakes and waders in the truck bed and headed to the clam beds. Unlike soft shell clams, which require low tide to locate and dig, chowder clams (quahogs) have a hard shell and live near the surface of the sandy bottom, so they can be harvested with any tide by wading and raking the bottom. We were successful in gathering enough quahogs to make a nice pot of clam chowder for dinner.

Epilogue. #1. No Fish Today. The next day I stopped by our local boat repair shop and ordered a new steering cable. My original assessment was correct, installing a steering cable is not something you can easily do while on the water. In fact, it was not that easy to do on land. I have never had another steering cable failure, and my conclusion is that when a boat is 15 years old corrosion will get places you do not expect and cannot see.

Steering problems can on occasion be anticipated. Visual inspection of steering lines, joints, and gaskets can reveal cracks and leaking steering fluid. You may also notice unusual sounds as you turn your steering wheel and increasing difficulty or stiffness in steering. Should these things occur it is advisable to fix the problem at your earliest convenience and not just keep adding steering fluid, which at best is a temporary solution. It is a pretty safe bet that if your steering fails it will be at a most inopportune moment.

#2. No Speed Today. It was a typically busy late June day on the water with bright sunshine and pleasantly calm seas. I was in Rescue

Getting Seasoned

Boat Three, the 23-foot Steiger, and had a disabled 24-foot Rampage on a hip tow alongside. I was just maneuvering it into its slip after a short offshore tow when dispatch called with another run. A 32-foot Fountain center console fishing boat was disabled between Block Island and Montauk.

Captain's Log: June 28. 14:00 hours. As usual I called the disabled vessel, let's call him Gofast, on my cellphone and verified his lat/long, which placed him in the vicinity of Southwest Ledge, a popular offshore fishing spot. He was still fishing and could have anchored but preferred to continue drift fishing until I arrived on scene in about an hour. Upon arriving I found Gofast to be in a good mood despite his difficulties because they had caught three striped bass weighing over 30 pounds each. His boat was a well-equipped high end performance vessel with three, 300 horsepower outboard engines. His hydraulic steering had failed. Wow, 900 horsepower all running well, except for the fact that they could not be steered! As the expression goes, "Gofast was all dressed up with no place to go."

In most cases when a boat is being towed its engine should be in neutral, and if it is outboard or inboard/outboard powered, the engine or leg should be in the down position. This assists in keeping the towed vessel centered behind the towboat and prevents it from veering left and right while being towed, which in turn makes the tow a little quicker and more fuel efficient. Because Gofast had three engines without steering that were wobbling left and right independently it was necessary to tow it back to port without the advantage of having the engines centered..

As I reached across the water and passed the tow hawser and bridle to Gofast he asked me how long it would take to get towed in. The distance was a little over 20 miles so I said that at seven or eight knots it would take about three hours, at which point he asked, "Did you say 70 knots and about 20 minutes?" Very funny.

He was still chuckling as I played out the hawser and took the boat in tow, adjusting the length of the hawser across the three-foot wave crests such that both the towboat and boat being towed were at the crest and trough of waves at approximately the same time. Sometimes if wind and sea conditions change it is necessary to adjust the length of the towline in order to keep both boats in synch. This is particularly true in heavier seas.

Captain's Log: June 28. 15:00 hours. We had been under tow for about an hour when Gofast called on the VHF. One of his two crewmembers had fashioned a tiller of sorts out of a mop handle and could he try to run independently to see if they could in fact steer the boat and move at more than eight knots. I slowed the tow, and Gofast released the bridle and hawser from his bow cleats and dropped them into the water. He waited as I hauled them back into Rescue Three then added a little speed and surged out in front of me, headed generally north and west toward Point Judith. At first he went well off course to the north, then well off course to the south, and then was gradually able to steer closer to what would have been a correct rhumb line (in this case, rhumb line refers to the intended course achieved by a sailing vessel that must tack left and then right in order to maintain headway as she sails, thereby averaging the left and right distance traveling on each successive tack) while now moving at about 25 knots. I called Gofast on the VHF and agreed to meet him in the Harbor of Refuge at Point Judith and then again take him in tow. There was no way, even with all that power, he would be able to steer in the busy narrow channel into the inner harbor, especially with a strong outbound tide.

Captain's Log: June 28. 16:00 hours. I sort of followed Gofast through the West Gap seawall opening and into the harbor, although my track was much straighter and hence a little shorter than his. We then reattached the bridle and now short hawser and I asked Gofast to leave his engines running in the event we needed a little more power to negotiate through the outbound tide in the narrow channel as I towed him in. I had called ahead

to the marina for a space on an outboard dock which they had, and Go-fast had called ahead for his mechanic to meet them at the dock. Once through the channel with a little assist from his 900 horsepower, I moved Gofast from a stern tow to Rescue Three's port hip and quickly slipped him into the open space between two large boats already on the dock with about six feet to spare. Whew! Another boat in safely.

Gofast handed me a very generous tip, again never solicited but always appreciated, and I cast off and called dispatch. "Dispatch, Dispatch, Rescue Boat Three, RTB," and got the welcome response, "Roger Rescue Three. RTB."

Epilogue. #2. No Speed Today. Gofast's mechanic brought along a new hydraulic steering pump and was able to make repairs right at the dock so Gofast was able to get underway again that same day. This is not always possible as steering is critical for a boat, and repairs can be time consuming. Gofast learned that all the power in the world is not helpful without steering, and as Captain Bob related in story #1 "No Fish Today," being alone without steering is even more challenging. Captain Bob also realized that it is not practical to bring along every tool and spare steering part that might be necessary for underway repair. An alternative to the tow would have been for Rescue Boat to transport the mechanic out to the boat at sea, but in that situation there is no guarantee he would have all the parts he needed, nor in fact that he could repair it while bobbing around on the waves, in which case the boat would need to be towed in anyway.

Captain's Note. Steering a boat is a study unto itself. Many twin engine inboard boats have the hydraulic steering pump activated by the serpentine belt on only one of the two engines. Should that belt break or the engine fail there is no steering at all, even though one engine may be running fine. Twin engine boats, however, can usually be steered by controlling each engine independently. Of course, this would not work with one engine inoperable because of a broken belt or some other mechanical issue. In fact, when maneuvering a tow in tight spaces with a rescue boat it is common practice to place both engines straight ahead and steer solely by manipulating the clutch and throttle of each engine independently.

This causes the boat to turn in very tight circles, much like a bulldozer using its steering clutches to control each track independently.

If a sail or power-boat experiences steering failure it is sometimes possible to deploy a sea drogue or even a homemade one consisting of a bucket and line. Deployed from a stern cleat and depending on wind and tide direction and

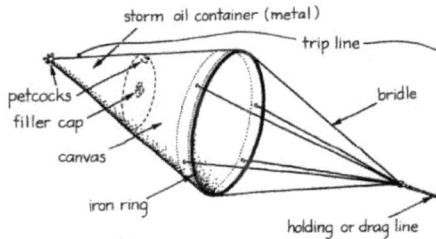

Figure 37. A commercial ship's lifeboat sea anchor. From *U.S. Coast Guard Manual for Lifeboatmen, Able Seamen, and Qualified Members of the Engine Department.*

velocity, such a drogue can cause your vessel to drift in a desired direction, and away from danger such as an impending rocky shore. New sea drogues are expensive, but in consignment shops they can be found for $25 or less, or you can devise and deploy a bucket drogue.

Steering problems do not discriminate between power and sail boats. I have cleverly managed to trap a lobster pot buoy and line between the hull of our 27-foot sailboat *Waterwitch* and her rudder, which brought the boat to an abrupt and surprising halt while still under full sail. I had to lower sails, anchor the boat, and jump overboard to free the rudder and to regain steering. If you remember Episode 2, "Pending Weather," the captain of a 36-foot sailboat managed to foul a sheet line in his propeller and thereby lose sail power, engine power, and of course the ability to steer. So, who needs steering…everyone with a watercraft on the water!

Episode 28

Captain's Log: *Disaster at Southeast Light*

Captain Hal Records

In this episode, "Disaster at Southeast Light," Captain Hal tells a rescue boat story in which classic and sadly common errors in judgment on the part of a boater very nearly cost the lives of five souls. It was Labor Day in New England and as with all holidays Rescue Boat was busy, and even with all four boats running all day, had what seemed to be a constant backlog of boaters needing service. Early in the season there is a spate of calls due to things such as water in the fuel, dead or weak batteries, failed bilge pumps, and other items related to winter storage. By mid-summer most of these have been resolved, but by Labor Day after long summer use, these and other maintenance issues, including steering problems, worn out O-rings and seals, and water pump failures keep rescue boat services busy. This Labor Day was no exception.

The weather for the weekend had been good and earlier in the day winds were south at 10 to 15 mph with seas at two to three feet. However, a northeaster was forecast starting later in the day and continuing for the next three days. This caused prudent boaters to head for homeport early before the wind increased and created unsafe sea conditions. We hoped that today would see most assistance activity early in the day.

Captain's Log. Labor Day. 16:30 hours. I was assigned to Point Judith Harbor and running Rescue Boat *Valiant*, a 26-foot center console with a pair of Suzuki 175 hp outboard engines, and had just returned from a four hour run towing a 40-foot Carver from Block Island to the border of our AOR near Watch Hill where a rescue boat from that area took over. The wind was increasing steadily all afternoon and was now 15 to 20 mph, with seas mostly three to four feet. Having refueled *Valiant*, she was resting comfortably in her slip as I reset her lines and cleaned up from the long weekend of service activity. I was looking forward to getting everything shipshape and heading home. A call to dispatch indicated the other rescue boats were still out but should be returning to base before dark. Tomorrow, classes at the university would begin and I would be back at school, preparing to start teaching on Wednesday.

I was getting my head into the transition back to the classroom when Captain Keith at dispatch called. A 22-foot outboard walk around boat was out of fuel and anchored near Southeast Light on Block Island. Oh… that was nearly 20 miles out in open water and I would be bow into the increasingly rough seas all the way. This would be a rough two or three-hour ride in turbulent seas because some boater didn't bother to calculate his fuel requirements, and because he had ventured out to sea knowing a storm was approaching.

Some people never consider the safety of the rescue boat captain when they put themselves in danger; they expect to be miraculously saved to go on their merry way. That, however, is probably why they call it "Rescue Boat Service" in the marketing brochures.

Captain's Log. Labor Day. 16:45 hours. As was standard protocol I telephoned the boater in distress, let's call him "Foolish," to confirm his position and provide him my ETA at his location. Foolish was nervous and with good cause. He and four passengers were aboard this small boat, the sky was overcast, and seas were building, but at least for the moment his anchor was holding. He had traveled all the way from Montauk to fish the area near Southeast Light and the new wind farm located there and he had stayed on fishing long after he should have headed to safe harbor. He was using what fuel he had to fish, not leaving enough in reserve for the journey home. Transferring fuel under these conditions would be challenging, and likely involve my tying a line to and floating a couple of five-gallon gas containers to him. On top of it all, Foolish's cellphone battery was low, and he was hard to hear. The only radio he had was a handheld VHF which had a limited transmission range. At 17:00 I exited the outer harbor, nosed *Valiant's* bow into four to five-foot seas, and headed for Block Island.

Getting Seasoned

Captain's Log. Labor Day. 18:00 hours. I was within one mile of Foolish's position and Southeast Light on Block Island, but I could not see him. His cellphone had apparently died, so I called him on VHF Channel 16. He verified his original position which now seemed from where I was to be awfully close to the island. Moving in closer to shore I could finally see him. He was anchored between a reef like ring of rocks surrounding the southern tip of the island and the rocky beach and bluffs of the island. Seas were now five to six feet, and as his boat rose to meet each successive wave it pointed at the sky. I could see nearly the entire bottom of his vessel.

    I confirmed with him that all persons aboard were wearing their lifejackets and told him that if his anchor should let go they should _not_ stay with the boat, but do their best to get away from it as the boat would surely be smashed to pieces on the rocks. There was no safe way I could maneuver *Valiant* inside the reef nor was it likely under the current sea conditions that I could successfully transfer fuel to him or transfer his passengers to my boat. I immediately called Captain Keith at dispatch, related the dangerous situation, and asked him to contact the Coast Guard for assistance and alert Block Island's first responders to the pending disaster at Southeast Light.

    Captain's Log. Labor Day. 18:15 hours. My VHF sounded on Channel 16, "Rescue Boat *Valiant*, Rescue Boat *Valiant*, Coast Guard Sector Southeast, switch and answer Channel 22." I kept one VHF on Channel 16 to stay in touch with Foolish and switched the second radio as requested. The Coast Guard could not establish communications with Foolish and asked if I could stay on scene to bridge the communications gap, which was my original intent. You may recall from earlier episodes that providing communications and rapid transport are two functions of rescue boat operations. A 34-foot Coast Guard Rib had been dispatched from New Harbor on the opposite side of Block Island with an ETA on scene of 19:00 hours, another 45 minutes. I seriously wondered if Foolish's boat could survive that much longer.

Seas were now mostly six-footers and the wind was beginning to whip froth and spray off wave tops as the Coast Guard Sector Southeast broadcast a Pan-Pan, "Mariners should keep a sharp lookout for a 22-foot walk around vessel in distress with five POB in the vicinity of Southeast Light. Render assistance if possible and notify Sector Southeast of any sighting." There was no response to this Pan-Pan, and not surprisingly as there were no other boats or good Samaritans to be seen in the area.

My challenge aboard Rescue Boat *Valiant* was now to "keep the open side up" while holding position outside the reef, and as close to Foolish as was safe and at least until the Coast Guard boat arrived on scene. Miraculously his anchor was still holding firm and all the people aboard were holding on to the edge of the boat and whatever they could grab as their boat pitched and rolled like a rollercoaster. I would imagine at this point that they were regretting their decision to stay and fish a little longer in the face of the oncoming storm.

I could now see a vehicle on the island with flashing red and blue lights high above the surf line on the bluff and near Southeast Light itself. The local harbormaster and first responders had arrived and had a bird's eye view of the situation playing out in the sea below. The harbormaster was on a VHF and speaking with me and CG3649, the responding Coast Guard RIB.

Captain's Log. Labor Day. 19:00 hours. My VHF again sounded on Channel 22 as the Coast Guard vessel came into view, traveling at a good speed and throwing considerable spray from his bow. "Rescue Boat *Valiant*, Rescue Boat *Valiant*. CG3649. What is your status?"

I responded, "I am holding position, and the vessel in distress is inside a row of rocks and between me and the island." CG3649 came within hailing distance and, still moving, quickly headed directly for Foolish, apparently not seeing the rocks that lay just below the breaking waves directly in front of him. As I keyed the radio to warn him, he abruptly stopped and began backing down hard. A less stalwart boat with a less capable driver would have been sunk by the six-foot waves now washing over the stern, the entire boat, and her outboard engines. Miraculously and skillfully, the helmsman managed to rotate the boat into the trough to regain control and then moved seaward away from the rocks.

At this point the harbormaster high on the cliff near the lighthouse radioed CG3649 and said there was a gap in the rock line about 200 yards to the south where it would be possible for them to get inside and then move back to the north to reach Foolish, thereby running inside a parallel to the line of rocks. CG3649 proceeded to do this, but stopped about 50 feet short of Foolish's boat, evidently concerned with the depth of the water. At this point they used what appeared to be a monkey's fist (a very strong, small diameter line with a tightly wound ball about the size of your fist at the end of it) to heave a line to Foolish and had him secure it to a stern cleat. Rather than edging their way closer they began to back down, thereby pulling the distressed vessel which was still anchored nose to the sea into the trough parallel to the waves.

Had the anchor line parted they may have been able to pull the distressed vessel backwards toward the gap in the reef, but the anchor held, and the line did not part. Foolish had good ground tackle. What did happen was scary. As CG3649 continued to apply pressure in reverse, the distressed vessel was pulled abruptly underwater and tossed all five passengers into the roiling sea.

Once again, the skills of the Coast Guard boat's helmsman came into play as he immediately ran his boat right into the middle of the five boaters swimming for their lives. His four crew members grabbed for the swimmers however they could and literally dragged them over the RIB's sponsons (tubes) one by one until all five were aboard. The helmsman then skillfully and carefully backed, turned, and edged his way south, returning to the gap in the reef. He then swung his nose into the sea,

184

leaving Foolish's now sunken boat to fate. When he cleared the reef, I called him on the VHF and offered to assist with transport of survivors if needed. He said he could manage to transport all five and that emergency medical teams were standing by in Old Harbor, Block Island. His last transmission to me was, "Thank you Rescue Boat *Valiant* for standing by and for your assistance, CG3649 out."

Captain's Log. Labor Day. 19:30 hours. I had been able to keep the "open side up" throughout the entire rescue by constantly maneuvering amongst the waves, so now the challenge was simply to get home safely running in the wind and rain. I radioed dispatch "Rescue Boat *Valiant*, Rescue Boat *Valiant*, RTB," and got the welcome response, "Roger that Rescue Boat *Valiant*. RTB."

I ran parallel to CG3649 until he turned west toward Old Harbor, then kept the seas on my starboard quarter all the way back to Point Judith. While on route I heard the VHF message, "Coast Guard Sector Southeast. Pan-Pan of 18:15 hours cancelled. Vessel has been assisted. Coast Guard out." Yes, the vessel sank and would likely be ground into fiberglass pulp on the rocks below Southeast Light before morning, but more importantly five souls were saved from certain injury, perhaps even death by being dashed on the rocky coastline.

Epilogue. I did not learn the specific fate of the boaters but on the next day there was no report of the incident in the press, so I presumed that any injuries were minor in nature. I was incredibly happy and relieved to get out of the angry seas and back into the welcome protection of West Gap in the  Harbor of Refuge. I slipped through the narrow channel into Galilee, backed *Valiant* into her slip, secured the dock lines, and radioed "RTB" to Keith in dispatch to tell him I was back ashore.

Getting Seasoned

I then climbed up on the pilot seat and just sat for about ten minutes. I thought about the tradeoff between catching fish and putting your boat and passengers at risk, and while I understand the excitement of a good hookup, I also wonder about the lack of common sense and judgment exhibited here. Hopefully, in the future Captain Foolish will pay more attention to fuel use and weather conditions should he acquire another boat. I did have a good feeling about the rescue, knowing that I played a small part in bringing the stranded fishermen safely ashore. Yes, for sure, the job of a rescue boat captain is not for everyone. Why do I keep doing this?

Epilogue

Captain Robert Behling and Captain Hal Records

As Bob Hope used to say, "Thanks for the memories." We have enjoyed sharing these boating stories and fishing tales with you. Both Captain Hal and Captain Bob have had the opportunity to enjoy many wonderful and at times exciting boating and fishing experiences over the years. There is no doubt that these times on the water have helped to shape what and who we are. We have learned that a life of being on the water presents special challenges for anyone operating a watercraft. Remember, *the captain is responsible for his or her vessel and all that sail aboard her.*

We cannot overlook commenting on the important and often essential services provided by our law enforcement and first responders. The Coast Guard has an awesome responsibility, and they carry out their duties exceptionally well. Harbormasters, community police, fire and rescue services, and let's not forget towboat services, all risk life and limb as they perform their day-to-day work helping boaters.

For readers interested in expanding your maritime skills we encourage you to investigate and perhaps pursue a USCG captain's license. For those interested in going further beyond completion of your captain's license, we encourage you to look into becoming a rescue boat captain. There is always a need in the rescue boat service for mariners who have good boat handling skills, enjoy a challenge, and desire to spend time on the water while helping others.

We neither sell nor profit from the sale of tow or rescue boat services, but as can be seen from many of our stories, subscribing to such a service where it is commercially available is an invaluable safety consideration, provides you peace of mind, and at a price of around $200 per year is one of the biggest bargains in boating today.

Be safe out there, keep the open side up, and enjoy every minute of your time on the water. There will be many more stories to tell!

187

Glossary

AIS: This stands for Automatic Identification System using radio navigation.

Anchor Rode: A chain or rope attached to the anchor to be deployed to keep the boat from moving in the water.

Anchor Scope: The length of anchor line from the anchor to the boat. Generally, the more scope, the stronger the bite of the anchor on the bottom.

Anchor Windlass: A device used to let out or retrieve a boat's anchor.

Armstrong Bracket. An engine mounting device designed for outboard engines. It is mounted on the stern transom and one or more motors are attached.

Backing Down: This means to withdraw or back off. When used in boating it means to stop forward motion when connected to a tight towline and put the towboat into reverse to slack the line and release the pressure.

Bare Boat Charter: Renting or chartering a boat without crew or provisions. The renter is responsible for providing these things.

Bearing Buddies: Bearings are used to allow boat trailer wheels to turn without friction. Immersion in water compromises the lubrication; bearing buddies are a grease cap that you fill with grease under pressure. As the grease erodes from dunking your trailer, the bearing buddy grease moves in to replace it and help keep the wheel rolling free.

Bilge Pump: A permanently mounted pump located at the lowest point in the vessel hull that is used to remove water collected in the hull. Usually activated automatically by a float operated switch when the water level in the bilge reaches a certain height.

Boat Wake: The turbulence in the water forming a path behind the boat caused by the propellor turning and the hull passing through the water.

Bollard: A heavy-duty post often mounted on a dock, used to secure the mooring lines of a vessel.

Bow Rider Boat: See **Walk Through Boat**.

Bucket Pump: A 12-volt electric bilge pump with jumper cables for battery attachment and flexible water intake and discharge hoses. It can be contained in a five-gallon bucket and is portable.

Captain: A boat captain oversees the operation of a boat and the crew. Depending on the type and/or use of the boat, the captain may be required to be licensed by either the state or federal government.

Catwalks: Narrow walkways that allow a boater to move between the stern and bow of a vessel.

Center Console Boat: An open hull boat with the helm placed on a console in the center of the boat. The console holds steering, motor controls, electronic and other apparatus used in boating.

Claw Anchor: This anchor is shaped much like an open claw. There are no moving parts, it is simple to manufacture, orients well to the bottom, and is generally less expensive than other anchors.

Danforth Anchor: This is a movable fluke style anchor and is very lightweight. The flukes swivel and provide good holding power in sand and mud bottoms.

Dewatering: This is the process of removing water from the hull of a vessel. The removal of the water is generally done with the use of pumps.

Dewatering Pump: A device to move fluids that can be operated by hand, an electric motor, or gasoline motor.

Drogue: Also called drogue anchor or **sea anchor**. A device in the water and attached to the stern of a vessel to control direction and slow the boat down, making control of the boat easier.

Fender: A bumper used to absorb the impact of a boat against a dock or another vessel, usually made of rope, rubber, plastic, or even old vehicle tires.

Float Plan: Details of an intended voyage shared with a person on the shore.

Gill Bracket: An engine mounting device designed for outboard engines. It is mounted on the stern transom and one or motors are attached.

Getting Seasoned

Go Bag: A backpack or canvas bag containing water bottles, food, floating spotlight, handheld compass, jacket/raincoat, whistle, first aid kit, and sheath knife.

Hailing Channel: Channels 16 and 9 have been identified as radio channels for mariners making distress and safety related contact with other mariners or the Coast Guard.

Hawser: A heavy rope or cable that is used to tow or moor a vessel.

Hawser Pipe. A metal pipe through which the anchor rope passes.

House Battery: Batteries used to provide power to operate AC and DC devices on a boat. It is used to supplement the engine batteries, preventing them from being drained while the vessel is not under power.

Inboard Motor: This describes the placement of the motor which is inside the hull of the vessel. The motor is connected to a drive shaft which exits the stern of the boat and has the propellor attached. Steering is done with the use of a rudder rather than movement of the propellor position.

Inboard/Outboard: This is a vessel propulsion system where the motor is mounted in the hull of the vessel and is connected to a drive unit mounted to the outside of the hull. The drive unit includes the propellor and controls the steering of the vessel.

Kedge: A small anchor used for pulling a vessel along after dropping it some distance from the vessel. Also, the process of moving a vessel by repeatedly tossing and recovering an anchor.

Lat/Long: Latitude and longitude that form angles and intersect on a globe to pinpoint geographic positions on the surface of the earth.

Lift Bags: Rubberized bags that can be filled with air and used to assist in a marine salvage operation to retrieve a vessel or other items from the seabed following a sinking.

Mayday: This is a marine emergency radio call in life-threatening situations. It is broadcast by a mariner in distress, describing the vessel, vessel location, and situation.

Manifold: A device that has one input and several output pathways. A manifold is used in salvage operations to sequentially inflate lift bags.

Rescue Boat

Monkey Fist: This is a rope knot created by an over and under weave, often tied around a heavy object such as a small rock. It is tied to the end of a rope to provide a weighted end to assist in throwing the rope.

Motor Guard: When towing a boat there are often opportunities for collision with the towed vessel and a towline draping over the stern and getting tangled in the prop. Much like a heavy duty car bumper, the motor guard is a series of metal tubes that attach to the transom and protect the outboard motor from collision damage with another vessel, and may also prevent a towline from getting tangled in the propellor.

North Anchor: This is a movable fluke anchor and is similar in look and construction to the Danforth anchor.

O-Ring: A circular gasket that is used to create a seal between the engine's outdrive and the watercraft transom, preventing water from leaking into the hull. Also, any circular (usually rubber) gasket deployed to prevent the leakage of liquids or gases.

Outboard Motor. This describes the placement of the motor outside the hull of the vessel and mounted to the transom. Steering is accomplished by movement of the motor, which in turn changes the direction of the propellor thrust.

Output Air Compressor: A device that compresses air to a higher pressure to be used to inflate devices or operate power tools. This provides compressed air to a manifold for the inflation of lift bags.

Pan-Pan: This is a marine radio call to alert boaters that someone is declaring an emergency that is not a dangerous situation for the vessel or life threatening for people on board the vessel. This radio call is often used by the Coast Guard in situations related to mechanical issues.

Pillow Type Salvage Airbags: Inflatable bags used for buoyancy and support when performing refloating and salvage operations. These devices are measured in terms of lift capacity, such as 2,000 pound or 4,000 pound capacity lift bags

Plow Anchor: This anchor is shaped much like a farmer's plow and is designed to bury the plow into the seabed. It works well in sand, rock covered, and mud bottoms.

Portable Pump: Gasoline or electric driven pumps that are not permanently mounted in the vessel and can be moved from application to application.

Propeller Hub: The center section of a propellor used to attach the propellor to the engine drive shaft.

Rogue Wave: A random and very large wave that briefly forms on the open water.

Rhumb Line: Term used to plot the course of a boat maintaining a constant compass bearing.

Roller Sprit: A device on the bow of a boat that allows the anchor line to travel over a roller to reduce friction as it is let out or retrieved.

Salvage: Salvage is the process of recovering a vessel or cargo after a maritime casualty. Refloating, towing, making repairs, protecting the environment from petroleum and other spills and leaks are all salvage operations.

Scupper: This is an opening in the hull of the boat above the waterline and above the deck. It is used to drain water overboard that finds its way into the boat.

Sea Anchor: A device that is streamed from a boat to limit forward progress or control the heading of the boat through drag. A sea anchor stays in the water column and does not attach to the bottom and can be as simple as a five-gallon bucket on a line let overboard and tied to a stern cleat of the boat, also called a **drogue**.

Securite: This is a marine radio broadcast by the Coast Guard or mariners to report movement in heavy traffic or narrow channels, fog conditions, or notice of marine hazards such as debris in the water. This is frequently used by vessels such as towboats when towing vessels that have limited maneuverability.

Sheet Line: A line (rope) used to control the movable corner of a sail.

Ship's Log: The official record of events in the operation and navigation on a boat, usually prepared daily.

Side Console Boat: This is similar to a center console configuration except the console is mounted on the side rather than in the center of the boat.

Snatch Block: A block that can be opened to receive a line over a roller and is often used with a winch.

Rescue Boat

Soft Grounding: A grounding where you can free your boat with the help of wind, tide, wave action, or a combination of any of them.

Sponson: A chamber that is attached to the outside of a watercraft's hull to provide buoyancy and give the hull stability. Sometimes also called tubes.

Spring Line: This is a mooring line used to control and limit the forward and backward movement of a docked boat. The line is hooked to the boat's stern cleat and moved towards the bow to be hooked on a dock cleat. Or it is hooked to the boat's bow cleat and moved to the stern to be hooked on a dock cleat. This is also used between two boats.

Steering Clutches: Clutches that allow power to be applied or withdrawn to effect steering of a watercraft, in other words independently engaging one and then another engine and propeller.

Strut: A metal component mounted on the underside of the boat hull and used to support the propellor shaft.

Telltale: A stream of water coming from the back of an outboard engine while it is operating. When a telltale is present the water pump and cooling system is operating properly.

Tow Bridle: A tow bridle is a length of rope with a hook in the middle that can be connected to both sides of a vessel and hooked to a tow hawser, or water ski line.

Tow Post: The post is typically made of stainless steel and is mounted to the hull of a boat to elevate the attachment of a towline. This keeps the towline out of the water near the propulsion system and propellor of the towing boat.

Transom: The stern (rear) section of a boat hull that can provide support for one or more engines.

Trough: A channel that will carry water or a hollow between two wave crests.

Turning Turtle: When a watercraft capsizes or turns over, putting the bottom up and the openside down.

Ungrounding: Freeing a vessel that has impacted upon a sandbar, the seabed, or the side of the waterway.

VHF: This stands for Very High Frequency radio waves used in radio communications.

Getting Seasoned

Walk Around Boat: This configuration is similar to a center console with the steering, engine controls and electronics mounted on a console in the center of the boat. There is also a small cabin located directly in front of the console. Space is left on either side to allow walking around the console/cabin structure.

Walk Through Boat: Also called a bow rider, it has seating in the bow and a passageway between the side console seat and the other side seat to allow passengers to easily move to the bow.

Working Jib: The jib sail on the downwind side of the boat and under tension from the wind.

Zodiac: A rigid hull inflatable boat.

Photo Credits

Page ii: Hal Records
Page 2: bls.gov.
Page 6: David Mark from Pixabay
Page 7: Hal Records
Page 13: work.uscg.mil
Page 14: co.accomack.va.us
Page 19: Kevin Scott
Page 23: Hal Records
Page 27: PIRO4D from Pixabay
Page 29: Hal Records
Page 32: VivekdChugh from Pixabay
Page 37: fisheries.noaa.gov
Page 41: glerl.noaa.gov
Page 43: fisheries.noaa.gov bluefin
Page 46: wildlife.ca.gov
Page 47: Woodsilver from pixabay
Page 51: Hal Records
Page 55: Hal Records
Page 60: nps.gov
Page 63: climate.nasa.gov
Page 66: cnic.navy.mil
Page 70: Hal Records
Page 72: Public domain, Pixabay
Page 75: WhipaSnapa Charters
Page 79: Robert Behling
Page 81: ri.gov
Page 84: commons.gao.org
Page 85: Gregory Roose from Pixabay
Page 88: Hal Records
Page 89: OpenClipart – Vectors from Pixabay
Page 94: Kevin Scott
Page 96: 9699186 from Pixabay
Page 102: osvaldito66 from Pixabay
Page 107: Kevin Scott
Page 113: skeeze from Pixabay
Page 115: PublicDomainPictures from Pixabay
Page 122: Hal Records, Rescue Boat Three
Page 123: Hal Records
Page 130: idfg.idaho.gov

Page 135: Daina Krumins from Pixabay
Page 139: atlanticarea.uscg.mil
Page 140: fisheries.noaa.gov
Page 144:response.restoration.noaa.gov
Page 147: Adobe stock image 272527002
Page 152: Hal Records
Page 153: Hal Records
Page 156: Peter H from Pixabay
Page 162: Hebi B from Pixabay
Page 164: Hal Records
Page 170: Hal Records
Page 171: Hal Records
Page 171: Hal Records
Page 173: gsaauctions.gov
Page 177: Pixabay
Page 179: blog.response.restoration.noaa.govdisaster
Page 182: Martin Klass from Pixabay
Page 184: epa.gov
Page 185: Hal Records

Author/Mariner Biography
Captain Hal Records

Captain Hal is a native New Englander who maintains his primary home in a coastal village in Rhode Island and spends a good deal of time at his second home on the sunny east coast of Florida. He has over sixty years of on-water experience. He earned a 100 ton Merchant Mariner Credential/Master Captain's license, including Auxiliary Sail and Commercial Towing endorsements. He is a man of many talents and throughout his life has always looked for new personal challenges. He spent four years active duty in the US Navy, went on to lead a successful software startup company, shared his knowledge of information technology and business management with students as a university professor, and recently completed more than ten years as a rescue boat captain for a commercial towing provider, where he did over 1,200 combined towing, rescue, and salvage operations. Hal holds an MBA from the University of Rhode Island and a PhD from Cornell University.

Author/Mariner Biography
Captain Robert Behling

Captain Bob is a native of New York State, and has spent his career in financial services and university teaching in some of the greatest outdoor locations in the world. He has lived, fished, and worked in Seattle, Washington; the mountains of Oregon; the Boise valley of Idaho; the mountains of Colorado; the coasts of Rhode Island and Cape Cod; the Gulf coast of North Carolina, Florida, and Alabama; and the coast of Australia. Boating has been the key to fishing both freshwater and saltwater species, and he has owned and operated numerous vessels over the years, his favorite being a Del Quay Dory fashioned after the Boston Whaler. He now resides on the coast of Alabama, where he is a state licensed boat operator enjoying the bounty of the Gulf of Mexico and the local rivers. Bob holds an MBA from Boise State University and a PhD from the University of Northern Colorado.

www.ingramcontent.com/pod-product-compliance
Lightning Source LLC
Chambersburg PA
CBHW052041090426
42739CB00010B/1995